ONE O' THEM GIRLS IN BLUE

ONE O' THEM GIRLS IN BLUE

Pat Lacey

ISIS
LARGE PRINT
Oxford

First published in Great Britain 2010
by
ISIS Publishing Ltd.

Published in Large Print 2010 by ISIS Publishing Ltd.,
7 Centremead, Osney Mead, Oxford OX2 0ES
by arrangement with
The Author

British Library Cataloguing in Publication Data
Lacey, Pat.
    One o' them girls in blue. – – (Reminiscence)
    1. Lacey, Pat.
    2. Abergavenny (Wales) – – Biography.
    3. Great Britain. Women's Auxiliary Air Force
    – – Biography.
    4. World War, 1939–1945 – – Personal narratives,
    Welsh.
    5. Large type books.
    I. Title II. Series
    942.9'98084'092–dc22

ISBN 978–0–7531–9546–8 (hb)
ISBN 978–0–7531–9547–5 (pb)

Printed and bound in Great Britain by
T. J. International Ltd., Padstow, Cornwall

To Gladys and all my WAAF friends,
both old and new.

CHAPTER
ONE

A sleepy little Welsh market town was how most people would have described Abergavenny in the 1920s, but for me, it was just a splendid place in which to grow up. Ringed by mountains, but not ones so high you feel dwarfed by their grandeur, it lies beside the River Usk in the county of Monmouthshire which seemed, when I lived there, not to know if it belonged to Wales or England.

The mountains are gentle, softly-rounded and tree-clad on their lower slopes — except for the almost incongruous shape of the Sugar Loaf that soars above the others and looks exactly like its namesake. For my brother, Bill, three years my senior, and I, climbing the Deri Mountain was our favourite Sunday morning walk with our father. First came a stroll up Llwyni Lane — in those days a magical place on a spring morning with sunlight filtering through an arch of hazel wands and the hedgerows thick with primroses and violets. Then came a couple of fields before we were scrambling up the hillside proper towards the oak woods that gave the mountain its name, "deri" being the Welsh for oak tree. Above the tree line, the ground leveled out and there were vast tracts of bracken criss-crossed by broad, grassy paths and dotted with dew ponds — and always the sound of larks in a sky that seemed perpetually blue. It must have rained sometimes, because Wellingtons were an essential part of our wardrobes, but I don't remember it ever actually happening.

I was born in Frome, in Somerset in May, 1922, but we only stayed there for a month before moving to Abergavenny. In those days, only the rich could afford to buy their own houses, so we rented the house on Hawarden Terrace, next door to its elderly owner who lived in a far larger house with a monkey puzzle tree growing in the front garden.

On the other side of us was the Howell family — a kindly, middle-aged woman called Ethel and her elderly parents. If ever my mother had to go out on her own for some reason and couldn't take Bill and me with her, we would be entrusted to Ethel's care and carefully inserted into her front parlour. I say "inserted" because the parlour was crammed with furniture and ornaments, so that we had almost to be arranged in order to fit. Once we were positioned at a large, round table covered by a chenille cloth with bobbles around its edge, we would be given the massive, dusty tomes of an encyclopaedia to leaf through. I distinctly remember an engraving of the suspension bridge at Conway, which I was encouraged to copy on to paper. Eventually, Ethel would appear, weaving her way carefully between sundry little tables, bearing glasses of fizzy lemonade — the gas from which always came down my nose — and slices of rather dry cake.

The parlour was a perfect example of the Victorian obsession with matching pairs. The mantelpiece, covered by another bobble-hung, chenille cloth, had pairs of elaborate ornaments arranged in perfect symmetry on either side of a large, gilt carriage clock. I particularly remember a pair of large, pink vases embellished with pictures of cattle grazing beside a river and rows of glass pendants — which I yearned to tinkle — dangling from their rims. Apart from the encyclopaedias, we were not, of course, allowed to touch anything, and it was always a great relief when my mother came to collect us.

Our terrace was opposite a railway goods yard, and Bill would assiduously record the numbers of all the engines that shunted up and down the tracks. Because I always copied what he did, if at all possible, I did the same, but privately thought it a great waste of time.

One of our most prized possessions was a wind-up gramophone, but we'd only ever been able to get our hands on the one record; on one side was a choir boy singing "Oh for the Wings of a Dove" and the choir of St Martin in the Fields singing hymns on the other. The second, for some reason, I called "Clowns in Clover" which my parents found exquisitely funny.

Every Sunday morning, my father would take my brother round the corner to morning service at Christ Church, a small, tin-roofed outpost of St. Mary's, the big Norman church in town. Eventually, after much pleading, I was allowed to go with them, as long as I promised to remain absolutely silent during the service. This, I managed to do and returned home to report to my mother that the hymns had been sung by a collection of "little vicars". Again, much parental mirth. I began to think I was the family wit.

I had few toys, but my favourite was a china doll called Bunty to whom I was devoted and used to take to bed every night until I was about fourteen. By then, her legs and wig had come off but I loved her just as much. In her heyday and while I was still being wheeled out in my pram, my mother would take great delight in dressing us identically. The same knitted jacket, trimmed with swansdown, the same, close-fitting bonnet. All my clothes were either hand-knitted or hand-sewn. Perfect strangers would stop us in the street to exclaim at my mother's ingenuity. There was another, larger doll called Paddy, who wasn't as "cuddly" as Bunty, and a beautiful two-footer called Peggy who wore a hand-knitted jacket with swansdown round its neck and was never played with at all, but simply gazed at. In retrospect, she was probably not a good buy since the greatest pleasure I had from her was during the run-up to Christmas when I would be taken to see her staring out at me from the shop window with her china-blue eyes and assured by my parents that Father Christmas would soon be bringing her to me provided that I was a good little girl!

Apart from Christine Jones — the only child of an ex-colleague of my father's who lived nearby — I never met any other children other than Bill, who had his own male interests. So I tended to make up imaginary people with whom I would have long conversations when I was out in the garden on my own. It was a big garden laid down to grass, and over the hedge at the bottom of it, our next-door neighbour had a chicken run made of wire mesh and often occupied by fluffy yellow chicks which, of course, fascinated me. One day, I amused myself by "feeding" them with privet leaves from a nearby bush until told to stop by my mother who assured me that they were poisonous. Imagine my horror when one of the chicks did actually die. For months, I was consumed by guilt until assured by my father that it would soon have been killed for the Christmas market, anyway.

I was a very shy child, terrified of asserting myself in any way and blushing violently at the slightest provocation. I was once dispatched to a party by my mother when I was about five. It was a wintry day, and I was wearing a very pretty, diaphanous dress, which she had made, with my white ankle socks covered by thick, hand-knitted knee-length "Wellington" socks, which I was supposed to remove when I removed my Wellingtons. My friend's older sister, of whom I stood in great awe, was supervising the arrival of the partygoers. I was petrified of keeping her waiting and decided, therefore, not to waste time by removing my outdoor socks and simply crammed my, by now, hot, sweaty feet into my indoor pumps and spent the afternoon in great discomfort, probably looking something akin to a fairy wearing hob-nailed boots. My mother, after I had confessed to her upon my return home, was horrified. What must my friend's mother have thought? Let alone the mothers of the other guests? In those days, one cared very much about the opinions of "other people".

Even getting me back home on that occasion wasn't straightforward. Along with several other children, Bill and I were crammed into a "dickey" — a sort of back seat in a car but open to the sky — for delivery to our various homes. When we got to ours, Bill got out, assuming, of course, that I was right behind him which, of course, I wasn't, and the car drove off with me still in the dickey and far too shy to protest. My poor father had to rush after us, waving frantically, and dig me out as if I were a forgotten parcel which, in a way, I was.

One of my happiest recollections of those childhood days is of my father telling us his "Rover" stories on a Sunday evening. We had acquired a family dog called Rover, a mongrel more collie than anything else and he, Bill and I and a fairy called Sunbeam were the principal characters. Every story began with Sunbeam tapping on my bedroom window early in the morning before our adventures of the day began. For years, I was enthralled by these stories, as was Bill, but for a lesser period until he deemed it a childish occupation and transferred his affections to Meccano and Hornby trains.

Naturally, I always wanted to copy whatever Bill was doing and occasionally — usually after my mother's intervention — I would be allowed to watch him playing with his trains. Occasionally, I would even be allowed to wind up the smaller of his two engines. I eventually decided to save my money in order to buy one of my own, and, after a year of hard graft, I'd

6

amassed the enormous sum of twelve shillings and sixpence (about 65p). On the whole, though, I was a miserly little creature (Bill was far more profligate), and when it came to the crunch, I couldn't bring myself to part with my hard-earned cash!

While I'm on the subject of money, pocket money was a very moderate offering. First of all, it was one Saturday penny, which eventually rose to one and a half pence, then twopence, then suddenly shot up to the princely sum of ninepence for me and a shilling for my brother. It was an unwritten rule that if either Bill or I were given money, we were to share it with each other. As I grew older, I augmented my pocket money by mowing the lawn each week for threepence a time.

There was little money spare for summer holidays, so we either went to stay with Uncle Ifor and Auntie Polly in Swansea or, more often than not, went on one-day, railway excursions. About a fortnight before my father's holiday was due, he would collect a sheaf of leaflets from the station, and we would pour over them to decide on our destination. Barry Island was a favourite; not only was there the sea and the sand but also a sort of pleasure park, where, for a threepence, tricycles could be ridden around a large enclosure for something like fifteen minutes. There was also a lake where children could take out little motor boats. Bill was once allowed to do this, but sadly, for some technical reason, got stranded in the middle of the lake and had to be ignominiously towed to shore by a man in waders armed with a sort of grappling hook.

One memorable day, we all went to Cardiff to see our first colour movie — *Ben Hur*. I'm afraid it was wasted on me; I was too frightened by the sight of all those sweating men being mercilessly lashed while they bent to their oars to enjoy the experience. For me, the outing was made memorable by a visit to a teashop after the movie, where I was deeply impressed by my mother, who, in a very grown-up voice, ordered pastries with our tea. Until then, I had no idea that bought cakes were called "pastries". My mother baked most of our cakes, but as an occasional treat, we would visit the bakery up the road — presided over by a pretty young woman called Miss Evans — and be allowed to choose "sixpennyworth of mixed" from a selection of coconut pyramids, Bakewell tarts and macaroons. Chocolate eclairs were outside our price range.

Our railway excursions always followed a fixed procedure. We lived some distance from the station and should therefore have set out in good time, but my mother always insisted upon washing up the breakfast dishes before we set off. This always meant that the rest of us, already booted and spurred, would nag her unmercifully until she'd finished. (I don't remember ever actually offering to help her!) We would then set off at a brisk canter, which must have been a bit tough on my mother who always wore court shoes with fairly high heels. However, we always made it just in time, and, while my father bought the tickets, Bill and I would dash out on to the platform so that we could watch the steam engine puffing its way towards us round the bend. Then, if we were lucky, we would find an empty compartment, haul ourselves up into it — the carriages were quite a long way up from the platform for short legs — and then, egged on by my father, sit at the windows and try to deter other passengers from joining us by pulling the most awful faces! This was a practice strongly condemned by my mother who would gaze steadfastly out of the other window and pretend that she wasn't with us! But we were in holiday mood, and the face pulling seemed largely to do the trick.

When I was five, I started school at St Michael's Convent. Thanks to my mother, I could already read and write and knew my numbers up to ten, thanks to the contents of the fruit bowl. I had also — and this has stayed in my mind far more clearly than learning to read and write — graduated from a chamber pot to a grown-up loo! I still remember the immense pleasure and sense of achievement I felt when I climbed up on to the wooden seat of the bathroom lavatory. Once I'd got the hang of it, I would simply sit there, whether I "needed" to or not! Clearly, I was well on the way to becoming an adult!

Mind you, this achievement wasn't in evidence on my first day at school. I was painfully shy, and though I didn't actually cry when my mother left me in the benevolent care of Sister Felicia, tears weren't far away. (My mother, I learned much later, did cry once she got back home.) Eventually, of course, I wanted to spend a penny but was far too shy to put up my hand. So, when my overwrought bladder could no longer cope with the strain, I spent it on the spot. I can still see the puddle spreading out along the bench — made of a peculiarly orange wood — towards my neighbour. She, of course, had no inhibitions and lost no time in leaping to her feet and informing the entire class that "Pat had done a pee!" Ignominiously, I was led away by a mildly remonstrative Sister Felicia to have my knickers changed. Clearly, it was by no means a rare occurrence as she had quite a little pile of them.

Since I could already read and write, I found the "infants' class" rather a waste of time, although my drawing left much to be desired. When we were told to draw whatever we wanted to, I always drew a war memorial with a cross on top of a plinth but could never explain why. Probably, it was because it was all straight lines, and we were allowed to use rulers, but I think Sister Felicia imagined it to be my budding spirituality. Occasionally, I would decorate its base with groups of rigid little flowers but that was as far as my imagination went in that direction.

After a year in Infants, I was deemed able enough to go up to Sister Octavia's class. This, I remember principally for learning all my multiplication tables off by heart and standing up to recite them, parrot fashion. I can still do this and have always found it extremely useful. Not so the very long poems that we also learned by heart, like Tennyson's *Camelot*, not a word of which I can now recall. Round about then, I started to learn French, for our Sisters belonged to the French order of the Holy Ghost with its Mother House in Brittany. One of their most annoying habits (no pun intended!), as far as we pupils were concerned, was to chat away to each other in rapid French.

However, I am jumping ahead. When I was six, we moved to a bigger house on the other side of town in Oxford Street, where Bill and I could have separate bedrooms. Until then, we'd shared a double bed with a bolster down the middle — a regular practice in those days. Not only was it a bigger house, it had a very large garden with a lawn, a large vegetable plot and a small orchard area with apple trees, gooseberry and blackcurrant bushes, a row of raspberry canes and a strawberry patch. My mother would pay us a ha'penny a basin for picking gooseberries and a penny for blackcurrants which took much longer. Needless to say, she picked the raspberries and strawberries herself! When the apple harvest took place, Bill would climb the trees and throw down the fruit. On one occasion, my father was hit in the eye by a particularly large specimen. Naturally, Bill and I crumpled up with mirth but he, of course was "not amused"!

The side of the house that faced on to the lawn had no windows in it and was therefore a perfect surface off which to bounce tennis balls — sometimes to the detriment of the flowers growing against it. I remember Bill giving a tulip "first aid" by wrapping a silver paper splint around its broken stem and hoping my mother wouldn't notice. She did, of course, but gave him full marks for ingenuity.

In the winter, Bill tried to teach me how to play rugby but was always having to shout at me for getting too far ahead. We also played cricket, one of our school sports until the nuns decided that using a hard ball was too dangerous — and it certainly was when I was bowling over-arm. Even the fielders had to run for it!

On Saturday afternoons, I went for a walk, either with Christine Jones, whose mother would come, too (mine didn't go in for walking except to town for shopping), or with my new school friend, Maureen Moxley. Her nanny — Maureen was an orphan and lived with an aunt who worked — accompanied us, and we always went back to her house for tea. It was a large house with a "breakfast room" which, in those days, was considered to be the height of "poshness". Chocolate cup cakes came with our tea, and these I adored. While I loved my mother's home-made flapjacks and jam buns, they came a poor second to bought cup cakes. We never used to eat them properly but would carefully nibble off the chocolate first before attacking the sponge cake inside. Sadly, when Maureen was eleven, she was sent to the Abergavenny Girls' High School and, from then onwards completely ignored me if we met in the street. Clearly, it was part of the High School ethic to look down on "Convent" girls. Her house, I noticed on a recent visit, is now a nursing home.

Sunday walks were quite a different kettle of fish and were always lead by my father. The walks themselves were brilliant and quite long, but my Sunday attire left much to be desired — at least in my opinion. For some reason, my mother liked me to dress differently from other children, and it was quite some time before I managed to persuade her to allow me to look like everyone else which, of course, was what I desperately wanted.

On Sunday morning walks in winter, my mother's obsession manifested itself in a fitted, Donegal tweed coat, white scarf and socks, and black, strapped shoes. Nothing wrong with this, you might say, although not exactly conducive to climbing over stiles, jumping streams, and swinging from trees, which is what I liked to do. But the crowning indignity, in more ways than one, was a black velour hat whose brim my mother had sewn up to make into a tricorne similar to that sported by Lord Nelson at Trafalgar. And while I'm sure it looked admirable on his Lordship on the quarter deck of the *Victory*, it left much to be desired perched on the head of a small child in the middle of the Welsh countryside. The crunch came when we were suddenly faced with a gang of small boys, one of whom pointed his finger at me and shouted, "Cor, look at that kid's hat!"

My father, of course, soon sorted them out, but he also reported the incident to my mother when we got home with the suggestion that my hat be returned to its original shape. This, to my great relief, she reluctantly agreed to do, but he could do little to remove her peccadilloes over my school uniform. I wore the regulation gym slip and white blouse, but instead of the black stockings that everyone else wore, I was sent to school in brown. Naturally, I loathed them. Fortunately, the weather came to my aid. It was very severe that winter, so it was inevitable that I eventually went sprawling on an icy pavement and ended up with the knees out of my stockings. Of course, my mother, with the help of a wooden "mushroom", always darned the family's socks and stockings which she'd usually knitted herself, but even she baulked at sending me to school with enormous darns in both knees. To my great relief, the replacements were black and just like everyone else's.

I had similar problems with my school girdle. For several years, I didn't have one — they were quite expensive — and had to make do with the belt that came with the gymslip. When — joy of joys — I was allowed to have one and was greatly looking forward to wearing it tied as tightly as possible around my middle with ends flowing free — just like everyone else — my mother insisted upon sewing the ends into a large bow with patent fasteners to fasten it. As far as I was concerned, the whole point of the purchase was lost.

The family's clothes were always bought by mail order, from Pontings — a large Kensington store whose catalogues were sent to my mother and which we all poured over when they arrived. Very occasionally, an order would be placed with Barkers, another, more up-market, London store. The local, Abergavenny drapers were deemed far too expensive.

My mother taught me to knit, and I managed to extend my wardrobe with several jumpers. I also made my school blouses from material which was purchased, at sixpence a yard, from a stall at the back of the market which was — and still is — a magnificent, covered building. Once I'd been shown how to make the prototype by the nuns, the results weren't too bad except that the waist bands — which didn't show under my gym slip — were never finished off.

Until I graduated from "combs" — a sort of vest cum knicker job — into "liberty bodices" — a sort of vest cum suspender belt — the neck of my undergarments tended to show above my blouse and I was always having to turn them in whenever I remembered. Navy blue school knickers always had white linings sewn into them in case the dye came off on our skin. They also boasted little pockets which were useful for keeping your handkerchief in.

Blazers were another bone of contention in our family. I longed for one with a school badge on its pocket but — again probably due to expense — this never happened, and I always had to make do with cardigans which were cheaper to replace as I grew in size but not nearly as smart.

I was always happy in my gymslip since I could put my hands through the armholes and yank up my knickers should the elastic be failing. I could also reach my knickers pocket by this method to get hold of my handkerchief. It was deemed unladylike by the nuns to reach it by simply lifting the hem of your gymslip.

My hair was always a problem. Bill was blessed with lovely fair, wavy hair, which he did his best to straighten, but mine was dark and dead straight. My mother couldn't bear this — her own was a mop of brown curls — so, from an early age, my hair was done up in rags every night and combed out in the morning. This was fine although rather uncomfortable, except that there would always be straight, short bits sticking out underneath the curls about which nothing could be done. This went on until I reached senior classes and put my foot down and just wore a straight bob with a fringe.

Re-reading what I have written about my mother's hang-ups over my appearance, I fear I may have made her sound like some sort of gorgon which, of course, was not the case. In hindsight, I'm sure she was only doing her best to turn a rather ugly duckling into a more attractive swan. The fact that photographs showed her to be a very pretty child wouldn't have helped. She must have been greatly relieved when the duckling grew up and turned into something that while definitely never a swan, did manage to sprout a few, reasonably attractive feathers. And since I loved school and was devastated when I had to leave, the hang-ups could not have blighted my young life.

Round about the age of ten, I was introduced by my father to the Public Library and thought it the most wonderful discovery of my life. Both Bill and I were lucky in that my father loved books and encouraged our reading at every turn. In those days, you didn't just stroll around the shelves to select your books. You were presented with a hard-backed catalogue in which every book in the library was listed. Borrowers consulted this catalogue and made a list, which was limited to three volumes. The list was given to one of the librarians — an elderly, white-haired gentleman and his middle-aged daughter who did most of the work and never took off her hat — who would then tour the shelves in search of your requests. Since this was my first visit, she decided which titles would be appropriate for me, and I went home with three books which, as far as I was concerned, were far too young and which I exchanged as soon as possible for more advanced reading. Kipling was one of my favourite authors at the time, and I repeatedly devoured *Puck of Pook's Hill* and *Stalky & Co.*

The school library, under the supervision of Sister Lucia, was growing apace and was a constant source of interest. But my regular provider of fiction was *The School Girls' Own*, bought for me each week by my father and *The Gem*, bought for my brother and passed on to me once he and my father had finished with it. I also had access to my mother's monthly magazine, *My Home*, which I found mildly interesting.

For about two hours each week, I revelled in the exploits of Betty Barton who occupied Study No. 12 at Morcove, a girls' boarding school. Her friends were Polly Linton, a madcap (Betty was the sensible one); Tess Trelawney, quiet and thoughtful; Paula Creel, very languid; Pam Willoughby, very "posh" and, for some reason, always murmuring "yes, well"; and Naomi Nakara, a dusky princess from some foreign clime who didn't always manage to get home for holidays. Although very happy at the convent, I yearned to go away to boarding school and have midnight feasts, which seemed to consist mostly of tins of sardines and cherry cake sent in parcels from home.

Hardly less gripping were the activities of Bob Cherry, Blake and Digby who occupied the pages of *The Gem* and lived in term time at St James's, familiarly known as St Jim's. They vied for my attention with Harry Wharton & Co. who lived in the pages of *The Magnet*, which my brother acquired by swapping *The Gem* with a friend.

Apart from their use of such expressions as "Good Egg!", "Well done you chaps!" and "Yaroo!" (used as an expression of pain), I now remember very little of their dialogue. But I do remember the code of honour by which they lived and one which my family — and possibly other, contemporary families — followed without deviation. Thus it was that when Bill boasted to us all that a girl in Woolworths had given him a ha'penny too much change, and my father assured him that she would now have to make it up from her wages, he immediately cycled back into town to return it to her.

"Well done!" said my father and said no more. But it was an incident that I have never forgotten, and I'm sure my brother didn't either. We were also taught never to lie and to be kind to the elderly and infirm and, basically, never to kick anyone when they were down and, of course, never to tell tales. My brother, probably much to his annoyance, was also taught never to hit a girl!

This last rule, most unfairly, didn't work both ways, and I frequently belaboured him; not that it did me any good. He was so much taller and stronger than me, he would simply put out an arm, and I would bounce off it. This, of course, made me even more furious and once, I became so infuriated, I threw a fork at him. Thank goodness I missed, but I was severely reprimanded by my mother and probably also received a smart slap on the back of my legs. My mother was the only one who administered slaps but always to the back of the legs. Even these could be evaded if you could leg it up the stairs fast enough and lock yourself in the bathroom before she caught up with you. It was rather boring sitting there long enough for one's offence to be forgotten, but it was worth it! Bill did once manage to escape by climbing out of the window on to the roof of the outside toilet and thence to the ground, but that was thereafter strictly forbidden by my father. And one didn't disobey my father!

To give my mother her due, she rarely reported misdemeanours to him unless she considered it really necessary; such as the time I flagrantly disobeyed orders and went with my friends to the banks of a fast-flowing tributary of the Usk near to our house and gave myself away by falling into it. Soaked to the skin, I was ignominiously taken home by my rather scared friends, who shouldn't have been there either. Once home, I was immediately stripped off, sent to bed by my mother, even though it was only eleven o'clock in the morning, and threatened with "corporal" punishment by my father when he came home. I lay there all day in fear of a sound smacking, if nothing worse. However, my father merely read me the "Riot Act" and forbade me to go near the river again — and I never did. Looking back now, I suspect that he was torn between upholding my mother's authority and not wishing to thwart my spirit of adventure. I think he was secretly rather proud of my occasional tomboyish activities and indeed nicknamed me "Tommy".

Bill and I did, I suppose, get on with each other reasonably well while we were growing up. He even referred to me, when speaking to his friends, as "Our Kid", which was one up on "my kid sister". As we grew older, our attitudes towards each other became quite civilized, especially when I realised that to have a good-looking brother was, in the eyes of my friends, quite an asset.

Those years before the war were a privileged time when we were allowed to walk to and from school on our own at the age of seven. But going straight home from school was never to be considered. There were always places to be explored, trees to be climbed, and hide and seek to be played. I feel sorry for children these days, escorted from door to door, often by car. We didn't have a car, nor did many of my friends, with the exception of Marjorie Dovey whose father was in Insurance and was given a car by his firm. An outing in that was a great thrill.

Marjorie Dovey also had a pony called Bess on which I was occasionally allowed to sit; I won't say "ride" since I bounced in the saddle — like butter on a hot plate, I was told by Bill — when Bess trotted, which couldn't have been much fun for her. However, she had her revenge by pursuing her own course under low-hanging branches whenever she had the chance. Absalom had nothing on me!

My only other form of locomotion, besides my own two legs, was Connie Lynch's bicycle. I wasn't allowed one for myself, because my parents — probably quite rightly — thought that I wouldn't be safe. Presumably I wouldn't have been allowed to ride Connie's either, had they known, but — what the eye didn't see . . .

I don't remember how I explained away the many holes in my stockings that occurred before I'd mastered the art, but I shall never forget the thrill of discovering she'd let go of the saddle yards back, and I was actually wobbling away on my own.

At weekends, watching school hockey matches (and later playing in them) and Saturday matinees at the Coliseum Cinema (two pence before two o'clock, four pence after) were my main diversions. Clark Gable and Errol Flynn were my heroes.

Occasionally, there would be extra Saturday morning piano lessons — probably because of an impending exam — with a friend who cycled about four miles in from the country, where her parents had a farm. While waiting for our lessons, we would be allowed to go into the parlour — normally used for interviewing parents — and pound away on the parlour piano at the current pop songs. "When I Grow Too Old to Dream" was a great favourite, as were "The Isle of Capri" and "Play Fiddle, Play". Deanne Durbin was our role model.

Peg was the only one of my friends who possessed a telephone. My excitement when she allowed me to ring her home from Abergavenny post office while she stood by me was intense. There was no direct dialling then, so I had to ask the operator for her number. Mind you, nothing happened for the first few seconds, because I had the mouthpiece firmly clamped to my ear!

However, all this riotous living stopped once I became seriously in to homework. Then, it was straight home and, after tea, incarceration in one of our two front rooms — with an oil stove in the winter — while Bill worked at his in the kitchen. Our other front room housed the piano which, in an unguarded moment, I had expressed a wish to learn. My delighted parents immediately bought me a piano for my birthday and were put out when I expressed no gratitude whatsoever and was, indeed, quite resentful. A piano was a piece of furniture wasn't it? And would have been bought anyway. My father always kept a meticulous record of all household purchases in a notebook and never threw it away. Years later, when I was clearing out his bureau after his death, I discovered that the piano had cost the enormous sum — in those days — of £41. Compare this with the £3 per term, they were paying for me at the convent and you will appreciate the extent of my ingratitude. However, one thing was for sure, after such an enormous outlay, daily practice was obligatory!

Also obligatory was a weekly half-hour of torture with Sister Agnes whose practice it was to rap her pupils sharply over the knuckles with a ruler whenever they played a wrong note. Wednesdays from 9.30a.m. until 10.00a.m. became a dreaded time, until I became more proficient. Then, I think, she quite liked me.

If I was in a good mood on Sunday evenings, when a fire would be lit in one or other of our front rooms, I would regale my captive family with a concert. If I was in a foul mood which, I'm afraid, happened sometimes, I would turn it into a scale-practising session until ordered to stop by my father! I was a little toad on occasion!

Sister Agnes was the only nun with whom I ever fell out. Otherwise, I loved school, especially when our only lay teacher — a Miss Florence Barclay — arrived and taught us English Literature. It was through her that I discovered the wonder of poetry and, I suppose, a keener appreciation of beauty in every shape and form. The glory of my mother's garden, particularly when the daffodils were in bloom, acquired a more vivid significance. And, at about that time, I began, with great regularity, to fall in love with all my brother's friends.

To them, of course, I was merely "Lacey's sister", to be endured on those rare occasions when my mother persuaded my brother to let me go with him and his friends on one of their sorties. I was a great trial to him, of course, since he had to look after me, and I was always the last to scramble over a wall or through a gap in the hedge — conventional methods like opening gates or climbing stiles were rarely considered. The arrival of one or other of his friends at our back gate, where they would click the latch in a lordly fashion until someone appeared — me, if I could get there fast enough — lent a certain piquancy to life. I was particularly attracted to one of his older friends who used to roar past our house on a motorbike every evening just after I'd gone to bed. I would sit at the window of my room just for the pleasure of watching his retreating back zoom up the hill. In the winter, it would be by the light of the gas lamp on the corner.

Although my father would not have earned a vast amount of money, our standard of living was reasonably good. We were well fed, largely due to the good housekeeping of my mother, although our meals did follow a strict pattern. Sunday was a roast which would be served cold on Monday with potatoes which usually had bits of black on them on account of having been boiled on the kitchen range, which was more economical than using the gas stove in the back kitchen. Tuesday was boiled chicken bought from the market and served again on Wednesdays; "boilers" were cheaper than the younger, roasting fowl. Thursdays, was rabbit stew, again the rabbit had been bought from the market and Fridays was fish followed by boiled pudding which I disliked intensely once the one spoonful of Lyle's golden syrup we were allowed, had disappeared. Fridays also brought a spoonful of Syrup of Figs and was my least favourite day. Saturdays, when my father would be home at midday, was always macaroni cheese with baked beans on toast for tea. Occasionally, this weekly pattern would be broken by liver and bacon or chops. It was, on the whole, a very healthy diet with lots of vegetables, grown in our large garden and fruit, also from the garden.

In 1936, to the great distress of both Bill and myself, my father was moved from his job at the Iron & Steel works in Ebbw Vale — whence he would commute each day on the train — to one of their works near Swansea, and the family had to go with him.

I was allowed to remain at the convent for the summer term, staying with a friend, while I took my

School Certificate, but then had to join the family in Swansea. I yearned to go back to the convent as a boarder, but there was no way my parents could afford it. In any case, they had Bill to consider. He wanted to go to University, preferably Cambridge, but the possibility of that in those days, when scholarships were rare, was even more remote. We must have been a right pair, festering away at home, no doubt getting under my mother's feet at every turn. Eventually, Bill took himself back to Abergavenny where he camped for the summer while he considered his options.

I decided to become a kennel-maid, until my father discovered that he would have to pay the kennels for having me! I also tried to become a probationer nurse in London but was refused permission by my mother — the only time she really did put her foot down — as she knew someone who had gone down that road and hadn't been able to afford a bar of soap — or so she claimed!

Starting school again in Swansea was an option I was offered but pig-headedly refused to consider. I longed for Abergavenny and my old friends and that was that. To my credit, I did try to pay my own way by embarking upon a literary career, but this proved abortive although it did give me something to do. When I was about five, my father used to buy me *Tiny Tots* magazine every week which, besides offering several pages of cartoon strips, also printed a short "Bedtime Story" of about 500 words in length. I decided to have a go at one of these and thus started an interesting exchange of correspondence with the editor. He must have been a delightful man because, although all my efforts were duly returned, the rejection slips always offered some suggestion for improvement — "try this", "what about?" or "do this" and always "try again". Since all my manuscripts were hand-printed with wobbly lines that always seemed to slope upwards — a sign of an optimistic nature, I've since been told — he really was most kind. Sadly, when the new autumn term started and I'd had no success, I abandoned him and his kind advice. Several years later, when I'd acquired a typewriter and there was another editor, I did submit another "Bedtime Story" and received the princely sum of twelve shillings and sixpence (new money, about 65p) so I would have had to write practically non-stop, with little time for school work, to send me back to the convent!

Eventually, I read in the *Swansea Evening Post* about a Civil Service exam for entry into the Post Office as a Telegraphist. I sent off for the syllabus and spent the summer of 1938 lying on my tummy in the garden studying from books acquired from the local library. My system was to work for twenty minutes then spend the next ten pouring over the pages of *Film Weekly* — Nelson Eddy and Alan Jones had now taken over from Clark and Errol. The system must have worked fairly well since when the results came out in the autumn, I was third out of a field of about thirty. However, only the first candidate was chosen so, feeling a twinge of sympathy for one, "J. Isaac." who had come second, I resigned myself to a couple of years at a Secretarial College in the town, starting the following spring.

However, a few months later, when I had forgotten all about it, I was informed that I had been accepted as a trainee telegraphist and was expected to report to Swansea Post Office in a week's time. Great jubilation! I was about to become a wage-earner! I went off to see Alan Jones in *Rosalie* in a state of mild euphoria.

Sadly, it was short-lived. I hated it! Apart from anything else, it was so noisy. I'd had the vaguest notion of what a telegraphist was or did and hadn't expected a vast room containing something like a dozen clattering teleprinters and a telephone switchboard — all manned by personnel, mostly female, who weren't supposed to talk but did!

"I'm not going to stay," I told my mother on my return home.

"Give it a week," she advised sensibly, no doubt with fingers crossed.

And at the end of the week, they gave me some money! Not a lot — seven and sixpence, in fact, equivalent to about 32p in present-day currency — but the Welsh Opera Company were visiting Swansea Empire the following week and I was able to afford three sumptuous seats in the stalls — *Faust, La Boheme* and *Madam Butterfly*, if I remember correctly. Grudgingly I decided to stay a little longer.

A telegraphist's job, I discovered, was to send and receive telegrams. One received them over the telephone through headphones while typing out the words on to telegram forms. They would then be transmitted over the teleprinter circuits to the major cities, like London, Manchester, Liverpool and Cardiff.

Typed out on keyboards at the sending end, they would emerge at the receiving end in the form of adhesive ticker tape which would then be stuck on to telegram forms. No visible record of the transmission would be kept at the sending end, so a high degree of accuracy was expected; numbers and any unusual words were always repeated at the end of a message.

Inevitably, mistakes were sometimes made. My biggest blunder was to send the wrong date for a funeral so that the mourners all arrived after the event. For this misdemeanour, needless to say, I received a severe reprimand from on high.

Training for the job, I was told, would last six months. There being nothing else on the horizon, I resigned myself to the inevitable and decided to stay.

Anyway, by now I had met up with J. Isaac, otherwise Joan, who turned out to be great fun and was several weeks ahead of me in the learning of touch typing. She was as keen on the cinema as me and able to relate, in great detail, the story of any film she had seen that I had not. It turned the routine of educating our fingers to send "the quick brown fox jumping over the lazy dog" into a much less boring business. We visited the local Plaza, Rialto or Grand at least twice a week and occasionally the Empire for a play where we sat up in the Gods for sixpence. By now, our wages had been increased to fifteen shillings per week.

There was a very strict dress code in the Instrument Room which was what our place of work was called. Bare legs and arms were not to be countenanced so we either wore stockings — rayon, one and eleven at

Woolworths — or, in summer, white ankle socks. Overalls or smocks were to be worn at all times.

At this point, post-office engineers, who wore brown overalls and were much more accessible, superseded my brother's friends in my affections. And so I implemented a personal enhancement regime and had my first "perm", where I was wired up for several hours and emerged frizzed up to the nines and terribly proud of myself. As a result, I was persuaded by Joan to attend the Waites Dancing Establishment, where I discovered that my sense of rhythm was practically non-existant. Boys would line up on one side of the room and girls on the other and Mr and Mrs Waites would demonstrate whatever dance we were supposed to be learning. After that, it was a free for all. For some reason, probably because he was roughly the same height as me, I was regularly commandeered by a fair-haired young man for practically every dance. Nice work, you might think, and ripe with possibilities — but not so. He would cross the floor, stand about six feet away from me and jerk his head to indicate that I should join him. And I, grateful not to be a wallflower, would get up obediently and join him. But never a syllable of conversation did we exchange. When the music ended, he would at least see me back to my seat but would then return to his own, until it started again, and the whole process would be repeated. I gave up after a few weeks, and I don't think Joan lasted much longer.

The most exciting event of all, perhaps, was the acquisition, at long last, of my own bicycle. I bought it for twelve shillings and sixpence — about 60p in new money — from the girl who lived across the road. It was a majestic "sit up and beg" affair that I christened George. From his superior height, I could survey the countryside in a lordly fashion while my friends were bent double over their racing handlebars. Of course, they did move much faster than me and frequently had to wait at crossroads if I didn't know the way. Round about then, I formed a brief friendship with a boy who owned a tandem, and we would whiz along with great panache and once actually passed a car on a downhill run. I remember that he had red hair and used to sing "To hell with Burgundy!" at the top of his voice as we dashed along. We must have been a terrifying sight.

Whatever the means of transport, the glories of the Gower Peninsula with its beautiful coastline almost surpassed that of the Abergavenny mountains, and I was reasonably content. I had also started to play the piano again, as I was now in a position to afford lessons. *The Moonlight Sonata* became one of my "*pieces de resistance*", as-well as *The Rustle of Spring*, which I would perform with great panache, especially the bits where hands had to be crossed. I was persuaded to play this piece at some Post Office function and wore a blouse with very full "bishop's sleeves" which lent itself well to the final frenzied dashes up and down the keyboard. Sadly, I was quite carried away by my perceived brilliance and ended up with a succession of deafening discords! People clapped, of course, but more, I suspect, out of a feeling of relief than appreciation!

And then the war came, and everything changed. To my everlasting shame, I welcomed it with open arms. Here was my opportunity to leave home — no matter that it was the happiest home you could imagine — and experience all the excitement and drama that was surely awaiting me "out there". Glamorous men in uniform now surpassed the "brown jobs". Naturally, I couldn't wait to join up.

But Fate, in the form of the Swansea postmaster decided otherwise. Apparently, the sending and receiving of telegrams was of national importance, and I was in a reserved occupation. So war was not to be the romantic affair I had selfishly imagined. Sadly, I resigned myself to a humdrum existence of blackouts and boredom as the "brown jobs" slowly disappeared into one or other of the Services.

My brother joined the South Wales Borderers, my father's old regiment and, after serving time in the ranks, was commissioned. Immediately, he became not just my brother, Bill, but an object of glamour, looking incredibly handsome in his uniform — not that I told him, of course! — and creating quite a stir among my friends when at home on leave. If we went out together and passed a serviceman of lower rank, I would glow with pride as he returned their salutes. It was as well we didn't live in London, or I would, no doubt, have had him walking to and fro in front of Buckingham Palace!

Rather less enjoyable was an episode that involved George. While I found it most enjoyable to bowl along the country roads on which there was very little traffic, cycling in town was a different matter. George, having fairly large wheels, was difficult to manoeuvre when being ridden slowly, and, because of my comparatively short legs, I couldn't remain sitting in the saddle while balancing with one foot on the ground. In those days, Swansea was a busy port, and the Post Office was located near the dock area. So I usually went to work on the bus. We lived in the suburb of Cockett, about three miles out. On this particular day, when I was due at work at one o'clock, I missed the bus, which would have delivered me in time. Waiting for the next one would have made me very late indeed and involve a fine and a reprimand which was not to be considered. I was still living down my unfortunate funeral debacle. There was nothing for it but to wheel out my trusty steed.

By skirting Town Hill, I was able to make a good speed along flat roads and, although I dismounted at busy intersections and pushed George across, I managed to reach Wind Street, where the Post Office was, without mishap. Free-wheeling down the slight slope, giddy with a sense of achievement and with several minutes to spare, I relaxed — too soon! I simply didn't see the middle-aged army major crossing the road ahead of me. The next moment, George, the Major and I were in a tangled heap in the middle of the road. I was quite sure I'd killed him. My relief when he picked himself up, retrieved his respirator from the gutter and told me, in no uncertain terms, that "you should look where you're going, my girl!" was enormous. Without waiting for my apologies — just as well since I was still speechless from shock — he went on his way, leaving me to hoist George upright and push him the remaining few yards to the office. Needless to say, I never cycled to work again!

Life in the Post Office became ever less exciting until the three consecutive nights when Swansea was blitzed. On the third night, to my secret delight, I was on duty when the sirens sounded. Seizing our knitting, books or whatever, we all trooped down to the basement which was well below ground level, and where a couple of teleprinters had already been installed for emergency use.

The building was near the docks area which, in those days was very busy and, judging by the many crumps, crashes and dull thuds that we heard, was one of Jerry's main target areas. Several "brown jobs" who were still with us, were on fire-watching duty and, from time to time, would report back to us with hair-raising accounts of surrounding buildings ablaze. Our building, they assured us, was miraculously still untouched. Eventually, when the Luftwaffe had done its worst and turned for home, we persuaded a couple of "brown jobs" to take us up on to the roof for a bird's eye view. Carefully avoiding our bosses, we were led up into what looked like the heart of an inferno.

We were completely surrounded by burning buildings. The sky — what was visible above the flames — was bright orange, mottled with great swirls of grey smoke. From the ground came huge jets of water directed on to the flames by the fire-crews below. We gazed and gazed and then, much chastened, went back down below.

Soon afterwards, the All Clear sounded, and we began the long trek home. Several of us, going roughly in the same direction, started out together, often diverted by wardens because of unexploded bombs or craters or because buildings were still burning and threatening to collapse. As homes were reached, our group became smaller and smaller. Finally, three of us arrived at a final parting of our ways to be met by a man who told me, quite definitely, that Cockett had been completely destroyed. Now thoroughly alarmed, as my father had recently been moved to London by his firm and my mother was on her own, I walked on. To find that Cockett was completely untouched. So much for rumour!

As I walked up our short driveway, I saw my poor mother, white-faced and visibly trembling, staring out of the window at the orange glow on the horizon. She turned and saw me and rushed to let me in. Then said, as if I was late for an appointment, "Where on earth have you been?"

Apparently, buses had stopped wherever they found themselves when the bombing had started and then completed their journey once it was over and had thus been passing the house, almost in convoy. And I hadn't been on any of them. It was now four o'clock in the morning and she'd been quite sure I was dead.

After that, war became rather more personal, and I wanted to join up more than ever. My brother, now attached to the Durham Light Infantry, had been home on embarkation leave and was now, we guessed, on his way to North Africa. I had always tried to follow in his footsteps. Now was no exception.

And then, to my great joy, the demand for service women must have risen, for I was suddenly told "to renew your application, Miss Lacey!" Needless to say, Miss Lacey needed no second bidding, and I was soon presenting myself down at the Recruiting Centre. It never seemed to have occurred to my self-centred, twenty-year-old self that I would now be leaving my mother on her own and, to her great credit, she said nothing.

Now, the only decision still to be made was which service I would grace with my presence. In spite of my brother being in the Army, the ATS was out of the question — khaki would do nothing for my complexion, and Air Force blue was only marginally more attractive. Besides, the caps of both Services were too much like a railway porter's to be seriously considered, and their tunics were belted and not particularly becoming to someone of a somewhat portly design. So —

"The WRNS, please," I told the girl at the Centre. Navy blue was always smart, and their caps were quite saucy.

"Do you have anyone serving in the Navy?" she enquired.

"No."

"Or the Merchant Navy?"

"I'm afraid not."

"Then the only jobs I can offer you are those of cook or stewardess."

Until then, I'd had only the vaguest notion of what I actually wanted to do — as long as it wasn't operating a teleprinter! Going to sea was unlikely, I knew, but perhaps I could be a personal assistant to some high-ranking officer. I was nothing if not ambitious! But now, my plans were being thwarted before I'd even started. For there was no way I wanted to be either a cook or stewardess. I've heard since that all enquirers were given the same alternatives in order to find out just how keen they were. Had I agreed to become a stewardess, say, I would probably have been re-mustered into something more amenable within a few weeks. But I've no idea if this was really true.

"The Air Force, then," I now suggested a trifle grudgingly. "As a Wireless Operator, perhaps?" I could probably manage to learn the Morse Code, and I might even end up in direct contact with aircraft.

"The trade you'll be given will depend entirely upon how well you do at the proficiency test," she said briskly. "Which you can take now."

The proficiency test was quite good fun, and at the end of it, I was told that I'd passed with high enough marks to train as a wireless operator. And if I passed my course successfully, I would have the privilege of wearing "sparks" on my sleeve. That, I thought, would do me nicely!

Next came the medical of which I can now only remember a doctor partially covering my ears with his hand and whispering from a distance of about six inches, "can you hear me?" I assured him that I could and all was well. All I had to do now was to await my call-up papers.

36

CHAPTER
TWO

I was to report to Innsworth, Gloucester on the morning of November 1st 1942. My travel warrant was enclosed with my reporting instructions and a memo to say that I was to bring with me a warm, serviceable dressing gown, slippers and sufficient brown paper and string to send home my civilian clothes once I was in uniform. Soon I would be in my smart, made-to-measure jacket and skirt. Shirts, no doubt, would be "off the shelf". The dressing gown presented a slight problem as I didn't have one. The only person in the Lacey ménage who had ever had one was my father who needed it for when he went down to light the kitchen range every morning and make my mother a cup of tea. The winciette pyjamas, which we all wore, were considered to be sufficiently warm if we had to visit the bathroom in the night. However, if His Majesty's government said I must have one, then I must have one, and a rather smart, camel-coloured, Wolsey-style model was bought. I packed it in to my fibre-glass suitcase along with the brown paper and string, my sponge bag and a copy of James Hilton's *Random Harvest* — I couldn't imagine life without a book — and waited for the big day.

At a particularly chilly dawn on November 1st, my mother roused me from a deep sleep. I lay still and longed to go back to sleep. Why on earth had I volunteered? I must have been mad! But my dear mother brought me a cup of tea, and I began to feel a little more cheerful.

Even so, I felt more than a little apprehensive when I eventually boarded the train in my best Harris tweed suit and even more apprehensive when I reached Gloucester station and tumbled out on to the platform, almost colliding with a girl who had just left the same train and looked even more worried than me.

"Innsworth?" I suggested.

She nodded. "Yes, worse luck!"

Her name, I discovered was Leila Grant. She had come, if I remember correctly, from Nottingham and had been called up — that is, she hadn't volunteered but had been conscripted. Joining up voluntarily would have been the last thing she would have done as she had just become engaged to an RAF pilot and desperately wanted to stay at home waiting for his next leave. The song which began "Give me one dozen roses, put my heart in beside them and send them to the one I love" — or words to that effect — was popular at the time, and she sang it incessantly during the weeks that followed. Fortunately, she had a nice voice!

We bonded on sight and between us managed to turn what became, for me at least, a profound culture shock into something that was almost fun. On Gloucester station, there was only time to exchange the briefest of biographical details before we were scooped up by a WAAF MT driver and put in the back of an RAF transport in the company of several other dazed-looking females, several of whom were in tears. Leila and I talked incessantly throughout the journey to Innsworth and, once there, managed to find beds next to each other in the Nissan hut that was to be our home for the next week.

The rest of that first day is now hazy in my memory, but I remember a pep talk from the corporal in charge of the hut, chiefly about how lucky we were to be joining such a wonderful Service as the RAF, the youngest and therefore the most dynamic of the three. We were in no position to disagree. At some point, we were given a meal of spam and bright yellow pickle and were told that our kit would be issued on the following day. After that we were dismissed and told to settle in. Leila and I went for a stroll around the camp and were faced with our first dilemma when we found ourselves confronted by a WAAF officer approaching on a bicycle. Did we salute although still in "civvies"? She settled it for us by grinning broadly and wishing us the time of day. Gratefully, we grinned back and wished her the same, adding "ma'am" for good measure. The rest of the evening was spent in writing home or, in Leila's case, to her fiancé. If you happened to have a telephone at home — neither of us had — it meant queuing indefinitely for the one public telephone box. Eventually, our nightwear was donned — the ubiquitous winciette for me, slinky, sophisticated, black rayon for Leila — and we went to bed but not, for some, off to sleep. There were several stifled sobs from around the hut, but I managed to remain stoical. After all, I reminded myself, I was there by choice.

Hardly had I closed my eyes, or so it seemed, than I was rudely awakened by a tannoy system above my head urging me to "rise and shine!", and the unshaded light bulbs spaced down the hut were switched on. How I yearned for my mother and a cup of tea!

But cups of tea were the last thing our corporal had in mind as she strode between the beds, telling us in no uncertain terms that if we weren't ready in twenty minutes when she would be marching us down to breakfast, we would be on a charge. And yes, we could be put on a charge, even though we weren't yet in uniform!

Rubbing the sleep from our eyes, we donned dressing gowns and slippers and joined the trickle of girls feeling their way — for it was still pitch black outside — towards the ablutions block, several freezing yards from our hut. There, a row of wash basins and an expanse of cold, wet concrete awaited us. Girls in various stages of undress, stood in front of them. This was neither the time nor the place for the shrinking violet syndrome. We splashed water — cold, needless to say — over various parts of our anatomies then, clutching our dressing gowns around us, stumbled back to the hut.

Minutes later, we were shambling in some sort of order, towards the cookhouse. Breakfast was pilchards on fried bread and mugs of strong tea. Pilchards were not my favourite food, but the tea was hot.

Breakfast over — at least we didn't have to wash up — we were marched to the Equipment block. I think

I've already mentioned my assumption that I would be measured for my uniform? That, arguably, was the biggest laugh of all in the process of turning Miss Pat Lacey, Post Office telegraphist, into 464870, ACW2 Lacey, P. J. Upon arrival at Equipment, we were each given a white canvas kit bag — the sort of thing you see sailors balancing on their shoulders when they're joining a ship in old war movies. This we proceeded to fill.

A wide counter ran the length of the huge hut. Behind it, were rows of compartmentalized shelves. Between the two, stood two rows of airwomen, one behind the other, and already running their eyes up and down our bodies in an assessing sort of way; rather as an enthusiastic undertaker might have done. First, as you might expect, came bras.

"Three large," pronounced the airwoman standing nearest to us and running an eye over Leila's ample bosom.

"Three large," confirmed her partner, turning to the shelves. Three white cotton bras, neatly folded, were pushed over the counter, landing neatly in Leila's open kitbag.

"Three small," said the assessing airwoman, transferring her attention to my smaller proportions.

"Three small, it is," repeated her sidekick. And so it went on. Vests, round-necked, white, sleeveless joined the bras. As did, stockings, lisle grey and suspender belts, cotton, pink.

"I can hardly wait," breathed Leila, "for my knickers!"

They were certainly worth waiting for. Three pairs of woolly stockinette, mauve for the winter and three pairs of silk stockinette, navy, elasticated at waist and knee, for the summer. The mauve jobs were called "twilights" and the summer ones, blackouts or passion-killers, presumably because the elastic would have curbed any lustful tendencies right from the start.

"We wouldn't be seen dead in those," we assured the grinning WAAFs behind the counter.

"You will!" they assured us. "Not dead but wearing them!" And we did. November, 1942 was a very cold month indeed.

Our actual uniforms were issued by the same method. "There are camp tailors," we were told. "They'll fix them, if necessary."

There were two skirts, two jackets, three shirts with detachable collars and one greatcoat. Shoes, we were actually allowed to try on. Caps, also. Again, it was small, medium or large and if they didn't actually balance on your ears or sit like a pimple on the back of your head, they were deemed to fit. I looked like an inebriated bus conductress.

Nothing was forgotten; collar studs, shoe cleaning brushes, clothes brushes, button sticks — even packets of sanitary towels. The last, apparently, were donated by Lord Nuffield, presumably on the advice of Lady Nuffield, and were very much appreciated. They must have saved us pounds. Also included, of course, was a gas-cape and a gas-mask.

We emerged from Equipment in a state of mild hysteria. What would our next rite of passage be?

Something, we were told by our corporal, who was waiting outside to collect us, called FFI. So, another hut, another row of waiting airwomen and, to our surprise, a row of empty chairs. The airwomen held combs, as it were, at the ready.

"Surely not a shampoo and set," breathed Leila in my ear.

'I'm afraid we have to check everyone for lice,' said "my" airwoman as Leila and I took adjacent chairs.

Lice! We nearly leapt from our chairs in horror and indignation. Where did they think we came from?

"Fifty percent of every intake," shouted a sadistic looking Flight Sergeant who seemed to be in charge of operations, "are lousy!"

We exchanged glances. Surely she was only trying to frighten us. But she wasn't. Apparently, FFI stood for "Free From Infection" and embarrassed girls were disappearing at a rate of knots and re-appearing several minutes later with their hair plastered to their skulls with some sort of ointment. The rest of us sat and waited, a captive audience for the Flight Sergeant who assured us that lice hop from one head to the other at the speed of light and were no respecter of persons.

Once re-united with our hopefully de-loused comrades, we were herded into another room where we were ordered to strip off down to our knickers and then to file past a poker-faced airwoman whose job it was to pull back the elastic and peer down at our tummies.

What, we enquired of each other, was that in aid of? The flight sergeant no longer being around to tell us and the poker-faced WAAF being far too occupied to ask, we were left to make up our own minds. The most popular theory was that it was a pregnancy check. Many years later — FFI's happened every month throughout my service career — I discovered that it was a check to see if our pubic hair was also free from lice. One can only hope that medical orderlies were paid extra for such an unpleasant task, but I doubt if they were.

The rest of the day consisted of packing up and sending home our civilian clothes and getting used to our new ones. Leila and I were lucky in that our jackets and skirts needed little alteration but we had no means of knowing what we really looked like since, wisely perhaps, no full-length mirrors were produced.

Next day, I made a catastrophic discovery — my colour vision was defective. This was discovered when we were given sheets of paper covered with differently shaded dots with a particular digit being picked out on each sheet in one specific shade. I was hopeless at it and trying so desperately hard that I was actually seeing numbers that weren't there. Matters weren't helped by the ubiquitous flight sergeant assuring me that she could see them perfectly. I could have killed her.

The outcome of the test was that I was deemed unfit to be a wireless operator as I might have to answer differently coloured glows and would not be able to differentiate between them. What, they enquired, would I like to do instead? I could think of nothing else and decided to come clean, as it were, and admitted to being a trained teleprinter operator. So I was re-mustered on the spot and told that I would eventually go on a teleprinter course to Cranwell in Lincolnshire.

"The Sandhurst of the RAF," I was assured by a WAAF officer who was, I think, a little sorry for me. But that cut no ice. Leila would be going to Compton Basset in Wiltshire for her course so we would be separated. Gloom and despondency!

However, that wouldn't happen for a little while yet as something called square-bashing was to be the next item on our agendas.

CHAPTER
THREE

One week after arriving at Gloucester, our intake boarded a special train for Morecambe in Lancashire. Those seven days had transformed us from apprehensive civilians into confident, uniformed airwomen, already trying out such phrases as "you've had that" meaning you hadn't and probably never would have; "gen" meaning news or information; and even "pranged" which was somewhat presumptuous of us since it was aircrew parlance for "crashed". "A load of old bull-shit" meaning rubbish or I don't believe it, was still to come.

In peacetime, Morecambe must have been a thriving holiday resort with hotels and guest houses crammed with holiday makers. Now, they were packed solid with airwomen of all shapes and sizes and from all walks of life. The transition must have caused even the toughest landlady to quail, and some rose to the challenge better than others.

Leila and I were lucky; our landlady was a "good sort". We were well fed and left to our own devices, as long as we behaved ourselves and kept the house rules. We were soon in her good books as we were quite happy to take our turn at washing-up and peeling potatoes and — an indication that we'd been brought up in a Christian household! — wore our WAAF issue overalls for the purpose. We must have seemed incredibly goody-goody to the others not so inclined.

The day after our arrival, the pavements outside the big shops were thronged with preening WAAF, gazing for the first time at their reflections in the plate glass. The Michelin man — the little man advertising tyres — was what I saw. Short and plump in the first place, layers of best-quality serge, topped by a greatcoat designed for serviceability rather than style, made me look like a little barrel. I had about as much sex appeal as a jellyfish! However, I comforted myself, the ratio of men to women in Morecambe at that time was probably something like ten thousand to one. Romance must wait until I was posted to a station. At the moment, it was enough simply to survive.

Corporal Scotcher was the corporal in charge of our squad and, like our landlady, she was "all right". By the end of the month, she had us marching up and down the front like professionals and even capable of intricate manoeuvres like "turning about on the march" or "eyes right on the march", while still maintaining speed and direction.

In the case of "eyes right on the march", I and several others had a tendency to march towards the person we were acknowledging instead of straight ahead, which was disastrous both for ourselves and the rest of the squad — and, of course, for the person we were saluting. However, this weakness was soon ironed out by Corporal Scotcher who could, if occasion demanded, produce quite a neat turn of phrase.

However, it wasn't all marching. Much of our time was spent doing PT inside the Winter Gardens in our vests and twilights. We were lucky, we were told, that it wasn't summertime, when we would have been performing outside on the front, in a similar state of undress, and much to the amusement of the locals.

When we weren't being physical in one form or another, we were being lectured upon such varying topics as VD, how to avoid it and what we should do if we caught it; gas attacks, what to do in the case of; secrecy, careless talk costs lives and general morale and behaviour and how privileged we were to be wearing the same uniform as the men who had fought and won the Battle of Britain. In between, we were vaccinated, checked for TB and, of course, checked again for lice.

However, we did have breaks each morning when we would mob the Salvation Army or YMCA canteens and drink hot, strong tea, devour biscuits or buns and, if we were lucky, slab fruit cake. In the evenings, we were usually too tired to do anything but stay in our billets and write letters or clean our buttons and polish our shoes ready for Corporal Scotcher's morning inspection. Occasionally, Leila and I would sally forth to a cinema though I cannot now remember anything we saw.

At the end of a month, we were deemed fit to be unleashed on to the outside world, and our intake was marched around Morecambe in a passing-out parade to the tune of the Air Force March played by a real RAF band which was, no doubt, imported from a nearby RAF station for the purpose. I do remember enjoying the march enormously and feeling very proud and patriotic.

On our last morning, Corporal Scotcher was presented with a minute box of chocolates and assured us in return, that we were one of the best squads she'd ever had — an assurance she probably gave to every intake. Anyway, we gave her three rousing cheers before passes were given out for seven days leave during which we would receive our posting instructions. There were many tearful farewells and Leila and I promised to keep in touch. (Sadly, after exchanging a couple of letters, we didn't, and I have since regretted this very much.)

Now, kit bags precariously balanced on shoulders, gas capes neatly rolled at napes of necks, suitcases in hand, we set off in our various directions, no doubt looking like Christmas trees and certainly, in my case at least, feeling strangely isolated after weeks of communal living. Also, I was by no means sure that I would eventually arrive at my destination of Swansea High Street GWR station, the railway network still being something of a mystery to me. However, I needn't have worried; the RTO (Railway Transport Officer) sorted me out — as they continued to do throughout the rest of my service life. Located on all railway stations of any size, they would not only route you to wherever you wanted to go but issue chitties if you missed your connection and were therefore late back to camp. They would also point you in the right direction for tea and a bun and a fire to eat them by while you waited for the next train. Later on in the war, I was to grow greatly attached to a certain Ladies Only waiting room on Crewe station where I spent many a night in comparative comfort while I waited for the milk train out to Warringon.

It was great to be home. Never had my mother's cooking tasted so delicious nor my bed so comfortable, and I greatly enjoyed meeting my old office friends and showing off my uniforn — even if it wasn't particularly flattering! One of the "brown jobs" was also home on leave from the RAF, and we enjoyed a riotous lunch, where we exchanged our different perspectives on service life. It was also, I remember, the first time I'd actually been invited out to lunch in a proper restaurant — I felt very grown-up and emancipated!

Halfway through my leave, I received a telegram telling me that I was to report to Perton, a satellite of Shawbury, near Wolverhampton, at the end of my leave. Once more loaded to the gunnels, except for the bus trip to the station when my mother very kindly carried my suitcase, I set off. Thanks again to the RTO, I arrived at Wolverhampton station at the scheduled time and was met by an RAF transport.

That night was the only time I cried into my pillow. I felt as if I was back to square one, among complete strangers and with no Leila to joke with. We were a mixed lot at Perton, accommodated in Nissen huts and waiting for various training courses to start all over the country. But of course, the despondency didn't last. There were a couple of other would-be teleprinter operators in the hut, and we were allotted to the station Signals section to acclimatize.

I don't think I ever knew exactly what went on at Perton. Certainly, it was small, quiet and non-operational. Most of my day was spent in the teleprinter cabin which was presided over by a friendly RAF corporal called, for some reason, Tosh. He had lovely red hair with matching moustache. Naturally, I lost no time in showing off my expertise on the teleprinter and probably became an insufferable show-off.

However, Christmas was looming, and on Christmas Eve, I was loaned to the cookhouse to help prepare our Christmas dinner. There, I was given a stool, a sharp knife and an enormous sack of sprouts and told to get on with it. I am ashamed to say that, apart from peeling potatoes, my knowledge of vegetable preparation was nil. However, I carefully removed the outer leaves off each sprout and then, for some reason known only to myself, cut each one down the middle. Next day, Perton personnel probably ate the soggiest sprouts they had ever tasted. Certainly, I have never liked them since.

On Christmas Day, I took advantage of transport laid on to take personnel to church, probably because it was something to do. I can now remember nothing at all of the service, but I do remember stopping outside a pub on the way back to camp. Until then, alcohol was something that simply hadn't occurred in my life, so it was a complete mystery to me why we were stopping there. It certainly wasn't an accepted part of other Christmas days at home. Anyway, the only piece of advice my father had given me when I joined up was never to go into a pub (it was over a year before I did!). So, wisely probably, on that occasion, I stayed in the transport along with several other WAAF and wondered at the strange habits of "other people".

On Christmas night, there was a Station dance attended by a contingent of Dutch soldiers who were stationed nearby. My dancing skills being still practically non-existent, I hadn't intended to go but was persuaded to by a jolly girl called Dot, who even tried to brush up my quickstep beforehand. Augmented by the Dutch, the ratio of men to women was in our favour and we had no difficulty at all in acquiring Dutch partners. The problem came if we wanted, as it to were, to exchange them. They stuck to us like limpets. And communication was difficult — mine spoke little English, and I spoke no Dutch.

"Loo!" I insisted at one point, thinking that that might prise my limpet away from me.

"Loo? Who is Loo?"

"Loo! Toilet!"

"Ah! Toilet!" He beamed mightily and proceeded to escort me there. I spent the next ten minutes sitting on the toilet seat hoping he would have gone when I came out. But not a bit of it! There he still was, dashing forward to claim me. Actually, I'm exaggerating here. Strictly speaking, he was, by now, quite incapable of dashing anywhere, having drunk far too many pints of beer. So, in fact, as the night wore on, he became ever more limpet-like. By the time it was all over and the band was playing God Save The King followed by the Dutch national anthem, it was taking all my strength to hold him upright.

"I see you tomorrow night," he murmured, pressing a slobbery kiss on my cheek. "Gate! Eight o'clock!"

"Gate. Eight o'clock," I echoed as I guided him towards his waiting transport.

I can only hope he stood me up, too!

Soon afterwards, on New Year's Eve, to be precise, I was at last posted to Cranwell for my teleprinter course.

CHAPTER
FOUR

The Sandhurst of the RAF it might have been in peacetime, but in the winter of 1942–43 it most certainly was not!

We were billeted in married quarters; that is, terraces of stone-built little houses with a living room and kitchen on the ground floor and upstairs, one large bedroom and one smaller and a bathroom. In peacetime, each house would have been occupied by an airman and his family. Now, eight airwomen were allocated to each house; three in the living room, three in the larger bedroom and two in the smaller. Although there was a fireplace in each room, no fuel was provided, and it was bitterly cold. At bedtime, it became the norm to simply remove our jackets, skirts and shirts and pull on our pyjamas and dressing gowns over our underclothes. On top of the blankets, we spread out our greatcoats. Some of us even wore balaclavas!

Teleprinter operators must have been in short supply at the time because there were two courses running simultaneously, one from 6a.m. until 2p.m. and the other from 2p.m. until 10p.m. If we were on the early shift, we got up at 4.30a.m. and were on parade at 5a.m. when, still half asleep, we would tumble out of our billets, line up in some sort of crocodile and march to the cookhouse. Since the camp was in complete darkness, one storm lantern would be held by a girl in the front of the column and one by a girl at the rear in order to alert passing traffic to our presence. Since no-one, except possibly the lantern holders, could see where she was going and the paths were always icy, it's surprising no-one fell and broke a leg. Perhaps someone did, and we never noticed! Breakfast proper was at eight o'clock after two hours work, but in the meantime, we were given mugs of hot tea and slices of fruit cake.

The classrooms must have had some form of heating or our fingers would never have been warm enough to manipulate a keyboard. So, once more, the quick brown fox jumped over the lazy dog, and I tried to keep a low profile. I had no wish to be promoted to a more advanced class and lose yet another set of friends. On the other hand, Cranwell wasn't exactly my idea of heaven, and I had no wish to prolong the experience either. Inevitably, it soon became clear that I knew what I was doing. So, well-ahead of everyone else, I was given my final test, passed out as an LACW — Leading Aircraft Woman — and was issued with two sets of propellers to sew on the sleeves of my jacket and my greatcoat.

Looking back, Cranwell had its good moments. Had I been a good dancer, I would probably have loved it, because the Saturday night dances in the Station Hall were a high spot for many girls. Cranwell was a big camp, and there were various signal courses going on for RAF personnel as well as WAAF so there was no shortage of male partners. I did go once, but after suffering the indignity of being pushed around the floor by one would-be Fred Astaire who, when he thought I wasn't looking, signalled frantically over my shoulder to a friend to rescue him, I gave up. I even thought nostalgically of my Dutchman!

But I remember a hockey match — much more my cup of tea — when the WAAF was supposed to be playing the RAF. After five minutes, during which the RAF scored five goals, we were turned into two mixed sides and had a really good game. Even more enjoyable were the hot baths we were allowed afterwards, when I discovered several hefty bruises on my shins. But it was worth it!

It was during this match that I met Margaret who became a life-long friend, although I saw little more of her at Cranwell since she was in a different class from mine.

I and my buddies, like everyone else, would spend our evenings — or mornings, according to which watch we were on — keeping warm in the NAAFI or the YWCA. Occasionally, when we could afford it, we would catch a bus into Grantham for a meal and, on one never-to-be-forgotten occasion, to Lincoln, where I wandered around the Cathedral in a state of mild euphoria. It was the first cathedral I had ever been in — we were far more chapel-orientated in my part of Wales — and was I impressed! All the deprivations of service life faded into insignificance as I wandered up and down the aisles or simply sat, trying to take in the grandeur and magnificence. My only other cultural escape at that time was through the pages of James Hilton's *Random Harvest*, and I have always felt grateful to him for my ten-minute read in bed every night before lights-out.

The only other occurrence of note while I was at Cranwell was being "torn off a strip" — RAF slang for receiving a severe reprimand — by a WAAF officer. It happened thus. One morning in the cookhouse at 5.30a.m., when we were having our tea and cake, I went up to the counter for a refill of my mug and turning back, brimming mug in hand, met the full force of a pair of ice-blue eyes belonging to a WAAF section officer that, starting with my muddy shoes, moved slowly up my entire length, past wrinkled stockings, unbuttoned greatcoat with upturned collar, crooked tie only partly obscured by untidy scarf, to the hastily assembled bird's nest of my hair. "Ma'am", of course, looked immaculate! Making an abortive attempt to stand to attention — difficult when encumbered by a mug full of hot tea! — I waited in some trepidation. But not for long!

I wish I could remember all the words she used, but the important ones are etched on my soul. "Airwoman, you are a disgrace to the Service! Never let me see you in this condition again!" As if I were drunk and disorderly and lying in the gutter!

No doubt I murmured something like, "Yes Ma'am, no Ma'am — three bags full, Ma'am!" Or words to that effect before bowing my head in shame and slinking back to my colleagues who had been watching the incident with open-mouthed astonishment and indignation. How would she, we muttered, like to be roused from her bed at 4.30a.m. on a winter's morning to go to work? The fact that she probably had — albeit by a cup of tea from her batwoman — we rather overlooked!

So, one way and another, I was quite pleased to be shaking the dust of Cranwell from my feet, especially as I was given a week's leave, while I awaited my posting as a trained teleprinter operator. However, there was a major obstacle to be overcome before I reached home. The London Underground!

In hindsight, had I sought out the RTO when I reached Kings Cross station, they would surely have told me how to reach Paddington from whence the South Wales train departed. But even then, I doubt if I could have coped on my own, especially with all my kit. It should be remembered that I had never been on an escalator in my life. When Margaret suddenly appeared at my side and also bound for Paddington — she lived in Oxford — it was like a miracle. Her class had graduated on the same day as mine, but, of course, I hadn't known.

She was an old hand at the Underground, and we were soon on our way. At Paddington, we parted but in high hopes of meeting up again as we had both put down RAF Benson as our number one choice for a posting. She, because she would be near home and I, because I had always wanted to visit Oxford — the city of dreaming spires, and all that — and home was the last place I wanted to be! Except, of course, for my convenience, like going on leave!

CHAPTER
FIVE

The journey to Benson was comparatively trouble-free — there were no London termini to negotiate as I had to change at Reading for Cholsey and Moulsford. At Cholsey, I met an RAF corporal also bound for Benson and, as we waited for the connection to Wallingford, he filled me in on what went on there.

It is well-known now that it was a Photographic Reconnaissance Unit. Unarmed aircraft — mostly Spitfires and later, Mosquitoes — would fly over Occupied Europe taking aerial photographs of strategic targets. They were dangerous and lonely missions with the pilots mostly flying solo and relying upon speed and very high altitudes (around 30,000 feet which was high in those days) as their only weapons. I was suitably impressed.

On arrival at the camp, my mentor handed me over to a WAAF admin corporal, and I was allotted a billet. Signal personnel were in married quarters as it was deemed to be quieter for WAAF sleeping after night duty. Having been allocated a bed in an "upstairs front" and dumped my kit, I was taken to the cookhouse for a meal. And there, to our mutual jubilation, was

Margaret. We couldn't believe our luck; even more so when we discovered we were in the same billet.

Our first full day was spent familiarising ourselves with the station: Sick Quarters, Equipment, Orderly Room, Guard Room, Parade Ground, NAAFI, YMCA and, of course, the Signals Section where we met our bosses; Squadron Leader Jackson and Flight Sergeant Miller whom we were told to address as "Flight".

The teleprinter cabin was a medium-sized room with, if I remember correctly, four teleprinters and, leading off it were the wireless cabin (where I never, ever, saw anyone answering a coloured glow!) and — holy of holies! — the Operations Room. There was much friendly, too-ing and fro-ing between staff in the wireless cabin but hardly any at all with the Ops Room, which was a hallowed place. One never entered it unless bearing a signal. It was presided over by an RAF squadron leader who was the controller, assisted by a WAAF corporal. One of the corporals in our billet — there were always two to each married quarter — worked in the Ops Room. She was a very glamorous creature called Mickey, who was known to be on friendly terms with several pilots who also visited the Ops Room but gained access through a door other than ours.

When we first put our noses inside the teleprinter cabin, I was much shaken to see a WAAF who was seated at a teleprinter suddenly pounding it with her clenched fist and shouting, "Oh, bloody hell!" at the top of her voice. Apparently, she had just been discon- nected from whoever she was sending an extremely long signal to and would now have to type the whole thing again. Convent educated (so was she, I later discovered!), I was greatly shocked. However, within a couple of weeks, I was "bloody helling" with the best of them! But those two words, with the occasional "damn" was the extent of the expletives we used. On the whole, we were a well-behaved lot. Incidentally, the angry WAAF turned out to be one, Pauline Webb — but always called Paul — who was great fun to be on watch with. I think she probably came from a somewhat privileged background, but did her best to forget it. From what she implied, her family would have strongly disapproved of her friendship with an ordinary RAF "erk" whose job was something like that of aircraft fitter; vitally important to the war effort, but one where he would have got his hands dirty. War was a great leveler of social classes. Paul was eventually posted to London, and I've always regretted losing touch with her.

Meanwhile, Margaret and I were allocated to the same watch and told to report at 0800 next morning. There were four watches with usually four WAAF on each; 0800 to 1300, 1300 to 1700, 1700 to 2359 and 2359 to 0800. (Don't ask me why the hour of 2400 didn't exist! It still remains a mystery to me.) When we finished at 1300, we were off duty until 2359 on the following night thus giving us a thirty-six hour break. So Margaret and I were to be entitled to thirty-six hours off as soon as we'd started.

"Good show!" I said, "but what shall we do with it?"

"No problem!" said Margaret. "We'll go home."

"But your mother won't be expecting me," I pointed out.

"That won't matter," she said immediately. And nor did it. Mother of six children, one more, as it were, made very little difference, and she welcomed me with open arms, as she continued to do over the years. But first, of course, we had to reach her. Buses were few and far between, and anyway, we didn't have much money as we hadn't yet qualified for a pay parade at Benson. So we hitched.

I wish I could now remember what sort of vehicle it was that stopped for us that first time, but it was most likely a lorry. It usually was. We became adept at climbing up into the driver's cabin and squashing ourselves into what was often a very confined space since the driver often had a mate. There were no seat belts in those days, and there seemed to be no restriction on the number the driver could take. Sometimes it was a private car, but these were rare because of petrol rationing. But whatever the approaching vehicle, up would go our thumbs. On one occasion, it turned out to be an RAF staff car with a very high-ranking officer sitting beside the driver — I remember the "scrambled egg" on his cap shining in the sunlight. Predictably, it didn't stop as the RAF driver wouldn't have dared to without permission. However, as it sailed past, both Margaret and I scowled horribly at its retreating rear. Immediately, there came a screech of brakes and, somewhat shame-faced, we scampered after it. The corporal driver got out and came round to open the rear door for us.

"You're lucky," he hissed out of the corner of his mouth. "His Nibs doesn't usually do this sort of thing!"

We climbed in while His Nibs continued to stare impassively ahead. Throughout the journey, no-one uttered a word, but when we came to our dropping-off point, we did manage a tremulous, "Thank you, sir! Thank you, Corporal!" His Nibs still didn't speak, but the corporal gave us a cheery wave.

I once met a girl for whom Queen Mary — the Queen Mother of those days — stopped her chauffeur-driven limousine. But on that occasion, the Queen was already sitting regally in the back, so she sat beside the driver.

"Did you curtsey when you got out?" I enquired.

"You try to curtsy in a WAAF skirt!" she said. "But I did give her a little bob and got a lovely smile back."

Hitching to far-away places was rather a different matter; you could never be quite sure of getting back in time. I remember once, after I'd been at Benson for at least a year, hitching to London with another WAAF called Gladys on a thirty-six hour pass. We arrived safely outside a convenient tube station — Osterley, if I remember correctly — and then went our separate ways for the night, arranging to meet up at twelve o'clock next day outside the same station which was on the right road for Benson. The only problem was that we were both on duty at 1700 hours. But my somewhat devil-may-care companion assured me we would have ample time. "I've often done it," she told me airily.

As arranged, we met up next day and took up our stance at the roadside, thumbs at the ready. However, for thirty nail-biting minutes, nothing happened, other than a steady stream of vehicles that swept on their way, apparently oblivious to our presence. Even Gladys began to grow a little worried. And then, to my enormous relief, an American jeep came into view — and stopped.

It was quite soon after American soldiers had arrived over here and British service women were still a novelty to them, not that they wouldn't have stopped anyway, because Americans were very good that way. Where, they enquired, were we heading for? We told them. No problem! They were stationed just a few miles away. And, sure enough, they delivered us, with minutes to spare, outside the camp gates.

"See you!" they called as they drove away. And they did. Gladys actually married one of them, a year later, and, at the end of the war went off to the States as a G.I. bride where, as far as I know, she lived happily ever after.

But I'm getting ahead of myself; American G.I.s hadn't even arrived in the UK when Margaret and I arrived at Benson. We soon became organised and settled down into a pleasant enough routine. The folk in the village of Benson — about two miles from the camp — couldn't have been more hospitable, and the canteen they ran was superb. I particularly remember their salad sandwiches; a huge, china bowl was filled to the brim with locally grown lettuce, watercress, spring onions, tomatoes and beetroot and all mixed together into one juicy mass. The bread was always stained a delicate shade of pink from the beetroot. The canteen was staffed by mostly middle-aged ladies, many of whom had children in the Forces. One of them I remember particularly; she was older than the others and always wore her hat, a most imposing, toque affair reminiscent of those favoured by Queen Mary. I think she must have belonged to a generation that never did take off their hats outside their own homes except at dinner parties and, presumably, the theatre. Suffice to say that we found her quite enchanting and used to love listening to tales of her youth. She, of course, remembered the First World War.

The other eating place in the village was the KCB; a charming little café whose full name was Keep Countryside Beautiful. There, we would go for mid-morning coffee and toast — we couldn't afford anything grander — which we made last as long as possible. It had the added advantage of being a rendez-vous for Benson aircrew at whom we would gaze furtively from beneath lowered lids. They were all commissioned and therefore strictly "out of bounds" for the likes of us. We only knew them as names on operational signals.

Just outside the village, on the road to Wallingford, was the Riverside Café that specialized in large slices of home-made fruit cake. It was much quieter than the KCB, and you could dally over a pot of tea for as long as you liked. I spent many a happy hour there, reading a book if I was on my own.

A similar place was the Bullcroft canteen in Wallingford. Much larger than the Benson canteen, it had the added advantage of being open all day. Benson, of necessity, had to limit its opening hours to the evening.

All in all, it was a very pleasant life — until, that is, March 29th, 1943.

CHAPTER
SIX

Margaret and I were sitting in the mess eating our lunch. We were on a day off and had been down to the Section to collect our mail which we were now reading. There was a letter from my mother and I was enjoying it, chuckling over the funny bits. She wrote very amusing letters, filling them with inconsequential little bits of information about mundane things like queuing for sausages at the butchers, or the price of eggs or making an overall out of blackout material. She'd actually signed off in her usual way — "lots of love, Mops" and then added a PS.

"I've just had a letter from Bill's CO. He was killed in action on the night of March 20/21. We must be very brave."

I looked up and stared at Margaret sitting opposite me. "Bill's been killed," I said and burst into tears.

Margaret was wonderful. "Come on," she said. "We'll go back to the billet," and taking me by the arm, she led me out of the mess. Halfway back, we were suddenly faced by a squad of the RAF Regiment being marched to their lunch by a corporal whom we knew slightly. To avoid having to pass them — I was still crying uncontrollably — she led me firmly across ground that, for some reason, was sacrosanct and had been wired off. Strangely, I have always remembered this small incident; the impassive face of the corporal who knew he must keep on marching, no matter what but managed to give us one quick, concerned glance, has remained in my memory ever since.

Once back at the billet, Margaret sat me down while she went in search of one, if not both, of our house corporals. She found Joan, Mickey's friend, who immediately went to see the WAAF CO and managed to wangle me seven days compassionate leave. She told me afterwards that this had been difficult as the WAAF CO hadn't wanted to give it to me. People were being killed every day, she maintained and I should just "grin and bear it" — or words to that effect. But Joan had persevered and probably made as much as she could of my tears and that I wouldn't be much good on duty, anyway. So I was able to catch an evening train from Reading and arrive in Swansea just before midnight.

Walking home — about three miles — was no problem, and I set off. I'd walked about two thirds of the way when I heard footsteps behind me and turned to see my father who would have heard from my mother at the same time. I think we said "Hello" and probably kissed but then walked the rest of the way in silence, unable to speak of what was uppermost in our minds. But we held hands, something we hadn't done since my childhood.

My parents were pillars of strength, my mother particularly so. Throughout my life, she was always there in times of crisis offering a shoulder to cry on and words of wisdom when the tears had stopped. I shall always remember when she was diagnosed with Parkinson's Disease in her early sixties, and it was considered kinder — as it was in those days — not to tell her. I yearned to discuss it with her and pour out my worries about the future but, ironically, she was the one person I couldn't talk to.

As if to rub salt into our wounds, on the day after my father and I reached home, we received a letter from Bill which must have been written a few days before he died. In it he spoke of the desert being suddenly in bloom as the short spring season arrived and all manner of colourful flowers that covered the arid ground. He wrote too of swimming with his men in the Meditarranean and of the wonderful feeling of being immersed completely in water after months of its strict rationing. His last sentences were about watching a small boat with red sails silhouetted against the last streaks of sunset. Although we all three wept uncontrollably as we read it, in the end it was a source of great comfort. Bill was always scrupulous about writing home regularly and would practically order his men to do the same.

A couple of days into my leave, I decided to visit an old school friend, Betty Godfrey, who lived just outside Brecon at Talybont-on-Usk. It was an easy journey on a long-distance bus, and I wanted to talk about Bill with someone of my own generation who had also known him. My parents were obviously coping and, I think, welcomed the chance to be on their own with their memories.

Talking to Betty while we walked by the canal or the river was just what I needed. We knew more, by then, of what had happened to him.

It was after the victory of El Alamein, and Rommel was on the run from Monty's 8th Army but fighting all the way. The German Afrika Corps were entrenched at the village of Mareth on the far bank of the Wadi Zigzau. Bill's regiment was on the opposite bank.

He and his platoon had already been out on the previous night on the hazardous operation of mine-clearing and on the following night — March 20/21 — were ordered to attack. Bill deployed several of his men under his sergeant to give covering fire and led the remainder down the side of the Wadi. Apparently, he had reached the halfway mark at the bottom of the Wadi but was then picked off by a German sniper and most of his men suffered the same fate. The operation was doomed to failure from the start, but what the Germans didn't know was that, while they were fully occupied on their front, Monty had sent troops — New Zealanders, I think — around the back of the adjacent Matmata Hills to attack them from the rear. Overall, the battle was a success with Bill's lot being the sacrifice that made it possible. It was all part of the horrible business of war.

The relationship between sister and older brother in childhood is hard to define. By its very nature, it is bound to be intimate — up to a point. For I can't recall having any conversations with Bill that in any way could be described as "in depth". I suppose children, on the whole, don't. It was only after the war had started and he came home on leave from the army that we had anything like a serious discussion. I am sure that, had he lived, my own life would have been greatly affected by what he thought and, perhaps, advised.

Tall and good-looking, he looked quite devastating in officer's uniform, so it came as no surprise when he came home on leave and told us about this wonderful girl called Molly. She'd started her service life soon after war broke out as a FANY (Field Ambulance Nursing Yeomanry) which, much to her annoyance was later incorporated into the ATS. To give her added glamour, she was a motorcycle dispatch rider whose life-size, cardboard cut-out was used extensively in recruiting campaigns. When Bill went to see her, she would often meet him at the station on her bike and put him on the pillion!

"And by the way," he added nonchalantly, astride the hearthrug, when telling us about her, "her father's a brigadier. And don't you start, Uggy!" (Uggy was the nickname that, for some reason, he'd bestowed upon me.) But, of course, there was no holding me. I teased him unmercifully.

We eventually met Molly who turned out to be great fun and not in the least "stuck-up" as I had feared she would be. And the "Brig" was one of the sweetest, kindest men I've ever met and thought the world of Bill as, indeed, did his wife. He was, apparently, much impressed by the combination of Bill's prowess at Latin (his favourite subject at school) and his success at sport. It was rare, he maintained, to find both academic and physical talents in one person. And he was probably right.

The Brig was actually a brigadier in the Tank Corps and, by great good fortune, was out in North Africa at the same time as Bill and not that far away from him. A couple of days before Mareth, he had sent transport over and arranged with Bill's CO that he be released for a couple of hours in order to come over and have tea with him! Bill would have enjoyed this enormously, both for meeting up with the Brig and for the "Britishness" of the invitation.

Hearing what had happened, he apparently drove over to Mareth a few days after the battle and was able to take a photograph of the battlefield. By that time, Bill had been buried in a temporary grave and he went to the trouble of picking a specimen of each flower that was growing there — the same flowers that Bill had mentioned in his letter — pressing them in a spare diary he carried and sending it back to my mother along with the letter of sympathy he wrote. It was an action that epitomized the man and gave my mother much comfort.

After the war was over, I was able to go out to North Africa and find Bill's permanent grave in the small war cemetery at Enfidaville, a very peaceful and beautiful place surrounded by eucalyptus trees. But, for Bill, there should also have been the wild, Welsh daffodils he loved.

CHAPTER
SEVEN

An incident occurred in 1943, just before I turned 21, of which I was bitterly ashamed. At least, in the aftermath; at the time of the event, I was very excited. It happened thus —

It all began on a day off. I wasn't on watch until 2359 hours that night, the sun was shining and I decided to go for a walk. Going for a walk in wartime if you were in uniform was extremely difficult. First, the vicar stopped in his dilapidated old Ford.

"Good morning, my dear! Can I give you a lift into the village?"

"Thank you so much, Vicar. But actually, I'm out for a walk."

"Good heavens! Are you sure? My tin Lizzie's more reliable than it looks."

"It's not that, Vicar. I really do fancy a walk. But thank you, all the same."

"Oh, well! If you're sure."

A hundred yards further on, the chairwoman of the Canteen Committee screeched to a halt. "Going to the village? Hop in!"

"Actually, it's so kind of you but I'm out for a walk."

"Really?" In her busy life, a walk, unless to take the dogs out, was probably a long-ago, peacetime indulgence.

"Yes, honestly! But thank you so much!"

Next it was a tractor driven by an elderly farmhand. "Jump up behind me, missy."

"Thank you very much, but . . ."

"You'm one o' them girls in blue," he interrupted. "Can't have you walking. Just put your arms around my . . ."

"No, truly! It's such a lovely day, I thought I'd LIKE A WALK!" the last three words almost shouted, partly because of the noise of the tractor, partly because I was becoming a little desperate.

"Like a WALK!" Clearly, he thought I'd taken leave of my senses.

"That's right! But thank you all the same."

And I marched on, waving vigorously as he passed, to show there was no ill feeling. Anyway, I was rather proud of having been referred to as "one o' them girls in blue"! I smiled to myself, filing it away in my mind to pass on to my mother when I next wrote. Since Bill's death, I was writing almost every day.

On I strode and managed to get through the village and out the other side without further interruption. Eventually, I found myself striding happily between fields of cows and sheep. Just as I was wondering if I could cut across country towards an inviting-looking spinney of beech trees where I could perhaps stretch out and eat the, by now, rather curled-up cheese sandwich I'd bought in the NAAFI on the previous

74

evening, I once again heard the sound of a vehicle coming up behind me. Resolutely, I marched on. The vehicle passed me and then stopped. It was a Canadian staff car, driven by a middle-aged but still handsome, Canadian army captain. Beside him, sat a much younger but also handsome Canadian lieutenant. Both smiled hugely.

"Where you making for, honey?" enquired the captain.

"Actually, nowhere in particular. I was — er — just out for a walk."

Part of my brain registered the fact that I had just changed tenses. I had just declared that I was just out for a walk; but, possibly, no longer?

"Well, why not come along with us, instead? We've just got one more call to make and then we'll need help about where to eat."

I didn't hesitate. With a quick backward flick of my wrist, I abandoned my sandwich to the ditch and climbed in beside them.

They were both charming. I have always been a sucker for voices, and their soft, Canadian drawls were irresistible. When we got to the depot they were visiting, they left me in the car. "Now don't go away, honey!" they called as they walked away. As if!

While they were gone, I racked my brains for a suitable place for lunch. It had already been established that I was to go with them. We weren't a million miles away from Wallingford but the Bullcroft canteen was out of the question. But what about the George Hotel? An old coaching inn. I'd never crossed its threshold but it looked suitable, and it was certainly the sort of place Bill would have frequented. And whereas it was verboten for other ranks to fraternize with officers, these were Canadians, weren't they? And known for their democratic ways? I decided to risk it.

The George was all that I'd hoped for, full of oak beams and inglenooks and glinting with polished brass and copper. The men were suitably impressed. I can't remember a thing we talked about during lunch, but it passed very pleasantly. It was wartime, the menu must have been fairly straightforward and the cutlery uncomplicated. All was well until the waitress suggested that we have our coffee in the lounge and, assuming, of course, that I would be "mother", put the tray in front of me. I stared, aghast. This was no array of brown liquid already decanted into cups that I was used to. Clearly, the George did things properly. I was faced with a gleaming collection of cups and saucers, pots and jugs, sugar basins and spoons. Where was I to begin? Other than Camp Coffee — an essence that came in a bottle and was only brought out at home on the rarest of occasions, coffee hadn't been part of my upbringing. Did one put the milk in first? And which was cream and which was milk? And would my companions help themselves to sugar or should I do it? And did they, perhaps, take it black? Did one let the coffee stand or pour it straight away? Blushing painfully, I stared hard at the tray. I hadn't really wanted the wretched stuff in the first place! But I needn't have worried.

"Allow me!" said the young lieutenant. By now, we must all have been on Christian name terms, but for the life of me, I now can't remember what theirs were. "That jug's a touch heavy for you, I think. Milk? Sugar?" And he poured with great competence. I could have hugged him!

When, in my confusion, I knocked a coffee spoon on to the floor, it was he who immediately bent to retrieve it. I relaxed and continued to make the most of lunching in a manner to which I now felt I could easily grow accustomed.

Sadly, once lunch was over, it was time for them to head for home but they would take me back to camp first.

"Now, I have to come this way again tomorrow," said the lieutenant when they dropped me off on the Oxford road, just by the perimeter. 'Any chance of our meeting up again?'

"That would be great," I said.

"You say you finish night duty at 0800 hours, right?"

"Right!"

"So, how about if you have a few hours beauty sleep, and I pick you up just about here at 1400?"

"That would be brilliant! And thanks for lunch."

"Our pleasure!"

I started to walk around the perimeter towards WAAF quarters in a state of mild euphoria. So much so, I had to be flashed twice by the Control Tower before I realised it was me they were telling to wait because an aircraft was about to land. The euphoria lasted until approximately 1200 next day when disaster struck. It was like this . . .

Still in my exalted state, I forgot when going on duty at 2359 hours that a gas exercise was scheduled to take place at 0800 and that I should therefore have brought my respirator on watch with me. However, I didn't worry unduly. The relieving watch always arrived ahead of time. And sure enough, at 0745, the relieving corporal sauntered in.

"Off you go, then," she said.

It had been a quiet night with no flying and half the watch had been allowed to go back to their billets at 0400, leaving just me and the corporal-in-charge. At 0745, there was still nothing happening nor likely to, so, without even discussing the matter, both my corporal and I went, and I reached my billet with five minutes to spare before the gas exercise started. After making sure that someone would wake me at 1230 — thus giving me an hour and a half to get ready for my date — I sank into blissful slumber. Two hours later, I was rudely awakened by a hand shaking my shoulder.

"Pat, I hate to tell you this but you're on a charge at 1400 hours."

"What! Why?"

Apparently, five minutes after the corporal and I had left, the Signals Officer had strolled into the Section looked ostentatiously under the chairs and behind the door and remarked, more than a shade sarcastically,

"Bit short of bodies, aren't you, Corporal?"

Result — I was on a charge for being absent from my post without leave. My corporal was in the clear because she had been relieved by the incoming corporal. I, apparently, had not. But the saddest part for me was that I would no longer be able to keep my date. Instead of getting ready for it, as I had intended, I found myself being marched into the office of the Queen WAAF — a squadron officer with eyes like gimlets — under escort and without my cap; the latter, in case I tore it off my head and threw it at the Squadron Officer in a fit of temper. Someone, apparently, once had.

Having explained the charge, she fixed me with a steely glare. "As this is your first charge," she began — and I thought, hooray, I'm going to be let off — "I will only give you two days confined to camp. You will report to the duty sergeant for whatever duties she sees fit to give you. Case dismissed."

And I was turned about and quick-marched from the room. Ten minutes later, I was wandering around the station like a lost soul, armed with a sack in one hand and a spiked stick in the other and picking up any rubbish, like abandoned sweet wrappers, I could see. Since I was trying to look as inconspicuous as possible and had consequently adopted a hunched posture, thus probably looking like someone in an advanced stage of osteoporosis, I was considerably put out when I was hailed by a friend who happened to be cycling past.

"Hey, Pat, are you looking for paper to light a fire with? I've got plenty of newspapers!" Needless to say, I soon enlightened her!

Once I had finished that particular chore — not that anyone checked to see if I had made a good job of it —

I was given the job of scrubbing the duckboards in the Sergeants' Mess bathrooms. This wasn't too bad as I also took my sponge bag and towel with me and managed to get in an illicit hot bath. After that, the duty sergeant couldn't think of any other chores to give me so I was told to return to my billet.

"But don't forget to report to me at 1700 hours. And remember — no going off camp!"

Apart from feeling very upset because I hadn't been able to keep my date, I also felt bitterly ashamed. Even though I felt it wasn't really my fault that I'd been caught out, I still felt that I'd besmirched the family honour. What would my parents think of me if they knew? Thank goodness Bill would never know about it! I didn't tell my parents until years after the war had ended when, of course, they laughed like drains! Bill, I suspect, would have done the same.

Over the years, I have occasionally wondered if my life would have taken a completely different course if I hadn't been on that charge. Did my Canadian lieutenant actually turn up? And if so, and I had been there to meet him, would anything have come of it? Would I have gone to Canada after the war and become a Canadian housewife with rosy-cheeked Canadian children wearing cute little lumber jackets and speaking with that same heart-stopping Canadian drawl that I am still such a sucker for? I shall never know.

CHAPTER
EIGHT

For my 21st birthday, my kind mother baked me a cake. Unfortunately, she forgot to put in the sugar! The friends whom I'd asked round to my room for cake and cocoa (yes, honestly, not a single drop of alcohol had as yet passed my lips), kindly assured me that it didn't matter two hoots and wished me "many happy returns!" But they still couldn't manage a second slice!

It was soon after this that Margaret and I were cycling around the lanes — I had brought George up from home and she had a service issue bike — enjoying our day off. I was just ahead of her on a field path when I suddenly smelled lime tree blossom for the first time in my life. Perhaps we didn't have lime trees in our part of Wales. So overwhelmed was I by the scent that I braked sharply without any warning and the unsuspecting Margaret, immediately behind me, ended up in the ditch. Apologising and explaining, I helped her out of it. And then we both realised that just beyond the ditch was a hedge and beyond the hedge was a thatched cottage with scalloped eaves and a thatched porch and a yellow rose tumbling around its latticed windows. I was entranced. We didn't go in for thatched cottages in our part of Wales, either, or else I simply hadn't noticed them. Closer inspection revealed a high wooden gate set in the hedge and bearing the name "Cherry Trees". Standing on tiptoe, I could just see over the gate — more roses, blush pink this time, and a flagged path bordered with pansies. By now, Margaret was peering over my shoulder — she was taller than me — and agreeing that it was "out of this world".

We must have stared for several minutes but were just turning away and about to pick up our bikes when the porch door opened and a slim, crop-haired lady, probably in her late fifties, came out, smiling broadly.

"Hello! Would you like to see the rest of the garden?"

Would we! Our bicycles were left in the ditch and we were ushered through the gate and into a paradise of scent and colour, made even more captivating, perhaps, by comparison with the fairly austere outlook we had back at camp.

At the side of the cottage, two copper-leaved cherry trees shaded a small lawn and gave the cottage its name. Mrs Mac — as we were instructed to call her — led us round into the back garden. It was, by my standards, enormous. A wide grass path ran between wide, flower-filled borders, the left one of which was backed by a beech hedge and was a riot of colour with blue and pink delphiniums mingling with phlox of every shade and size and Sweet William rioting between.

"I'm afraid," said Mrs Mac apologetically, and to our astonishment, "that it isn't what it used to be."

"But it's beautiful," we protested.

82

"Look carefully and you'll see that it needs a lot of work on it."

Obediently, we looked. Sure enough, dock leaves were sprouting between the little red bachelor's buttons that edged the path, convolvulus was twining through the delphiniums and couch grass was everywhere.

"Occasionally," said Mrs Mac, "a couple of boys come out from the village but I'm always afraid they won't know the weeds from the flowers. I do what I can but I have the hens and vegetables to look after as well. And they're more important."

And she led us down the garden to where the path finished in a tiny spinney of plum and cherry trees surrounded by a wire netting fence. Beneath the trees, half a dozen hens clucked and scratched contentedly. Beyond them again, we could see the neat rows of a small vegetable garden. Cornfields stretched away into the horizon.

Margaret and I exchanged glances but said nothing at that stage beyond exclaiming at the extent of her labours. The inspection over, we were led into the cool confines of the cottage and introduced to Mr Mac, a tall, jovial man who had recently been very ill. His considerable engineering expertise was now channelled into repairing wireless sets for a local firm who kept him very busy.

Over glasses of ice-cold water drawn from a pump over the kitchen sink, we learned that they had a son called Gordon who was with the 8th army in North Africa. Before the war, they had lived in London and Cherry Trees had been their weekend retreat.

Could we, we enquired tentatively as we prepared to leave, help at all in the garden? The airfield was only fifteen minutes cycle ride away and neither of us minded getting our hands dirty.

That, said Mrs Mac, beaming all over her face, would be wonderful. But we mustn't feel we had to work every time we came. It would just be very nice to see us.

Later, we learned that, for some time, they had thought they would like to "adopt" a couple of WAAF and offer them the benefits of home comforts when they felt in need. It was our good luck that we had happened along when we had. Over the next two years, I was a regular visitor to Cherry Trees, more so than Margaret who, soon afterwards, became friendly with an RAF sergeant and so had other things to do with her time.

One of Mrs Mac's specialities was making Scotch pancakes on a griddle on top of her Aga when she had the fat. So it became a regular habit for us to "nick" a portion of margarine from the mess for that purpose. We didn't consider it dishonest since our attendance at breakfast — when it was put out — was minimal.

Occasionally, I would stay overnight at Cherry Trees if, for some reason, Mr Mac had to be away. Over supper, eaten in the kitchen, Mrs Mac would regale me with stories of their pre-war life in London. Jack Buchanan, I remember, was one of her buddies. She had had what sounded like a strict but privileged upbringing, largely inspired by a Scottish Nannie. Whenever she or her brother had wanted something, they had always had to try and make it first and if that wasn't possible, their pocket money had to be saved. This practical attitude made wartime deficiencies much easier for her to cope with.

A few months after we had discovered Cherry Trees, Margaret and I had one of our "falling out" touches. In hindsight, it was to be expected. We were living virtually in each other's pockets, sharing the same room, working on the same watch, spending all our spare time together. It was inevitable that, from time to time, we didn't always see eye to eye. So I moved out to another married quarter round the corner, where I settled in quite happily and became friendly with a jolly little Jordie called Babs who was a wireless op. on the same watch as me. Margaret chummed up with another WAAF called Gladys (the same Gladys who later married the American and became the GI Bride).

Looking back, it was rare for any of us to be a "loner". Occasionally, I would go out on my own, either by choice or circumstance, but usually we hunted in pairs. Right from the start, Babs and I had a somewhat stormy relationship. She had a very volatile personality, and we sparred constantly, but she was good fun, and I have fond memories of her on her bright blue racing bike, crouched over the handlebars like a professional. Her chuckle was infectious, and we had a lot of fun in between the squabbles.

We were friends when the first wave of "white flashes" hit the airfield. "White flashes" was the collective name for the aircrew cadets who were waiting to be posted overseas for training — mostly to Canada or Rhodesia — and wore white flashes in their forage caps.

They were the next best thing to aircrew proper, and we fell on them with great excitement. Journeys to the NAAFI, where they gathered every lunchtime, changed from humdrum visits for a "wad and a cup of char" to a sort of potential dating agency. I met up with a charming lad called David who had already done a couple of terms at Oxford while serving in the University Air Corps and hoped to be going back there after the war.

For the few weeks they were at Benson, David and I met up on every possible occasion. I particularly remember going to see the film *Dear Octopus* with him and Babs in the Wallingford cinema and afterwards eating chips — we probably couldn't afford the fish! — out of newspaper in a shop doorway. Why did chips always taste so much better out of newspaper?

I took him on one of my favourite walks up Wittenham Clumps behind Dorchester-on-Thames, and in return he took me into Oxford to visit his old college. It was a memorable visit; we went to see one of his friends in his rooms and afterwards dined sumptuously at the George restaurant.

David was particularly knowledgeable about birds — the feathered variety! — and could recognize many of them by their song.

"It sounds just like someone pumping up a bicycle tyre," he said of the great tit. And it did. I was suitably impressed.

The relationship had all the ingredients of a war-time romance, and we declared our undying love outside married quarters late one night. Unfortunately, our ensuing embrace was somewhat marred by the sudden arrival of the duty WAAF officer, whose job it was to make sure that all WAAF personnel were safely in their billets by 2300 hours. With gay abandon and a complete disregard for our finer feelings, she flashed her torch over our entwined bodies.

Hissing into David's ear "see you at the back door in ten minutes", I unentwined and, like a good little WAAF, went indoors. Ten minutes later, we resumed where we had left off in the shelter of the back porch.

When he went off to Rhodesia a few days later, we had every intention of spending the rest of our lives together after the war. My mother, I remember, was delighted.

CHAPTER
NINE

Whenever I had a thirty-six hour pass and was on my own, I went into Oxford and stayed overnight at the YWCA, an admirable establishment where one could have bed and breakfast at a very nominal rate.

Even in wartime, Oxford was a magical city. I usually began with a visit to the English Speaking Union canteen on Carfax. It was up a flight of stairs and over a shop, and it was always thronged with personnel from many different countries. If I could afford it, there was also the Copper Kettle at the bottom of the High. Then I would browse around the bookshops, making a very occasional purchase.

The main attractions were the college gardens; those, at least, that were open to the public. My favourite was Magdalen with its deer and enchanting Addison's Walk beside the river, its banks rich with wild flowers. Across the High were the Botanic Gardens where I had a favourite seat under a lilac tree. I usually followed this with a stroll through Christ Church Meadows and, if time permitted, a visit to Christ Church Cathedral. In the evening, there was the New Theatre or the Playhouse. I particularly remember seeing Michael

Redgrave in Christopher Fry's *The Lady's Not For Burning*.

If I didn't go into Oxford, I would often cycle to Dorchester-on-Thames and wander around the Abbey or take the walk I had taken with David, over the fields, across the river at Day's Lock and up into the village of Long Wittenham. Then there was the obligatory climb up the nearest of the two Wittenham Clumps, originally the site of a Roman encampment and now crowned with ancient elms. There, I would lean against one of the tree trunks and gaze out at the airfield — several miles away — with the tree-clad Chilterns rising behind. Nearer to me, across the fields I had just walked through, the red and grey roofs of Dorchester village straggled beside the river.

When Margaret and I were having one of our reconciliations (which was more often than not, I may say!), she would take me on cycle rides to other villages that she knew. Clifton Hampden was a favourite but one that, ideally, should be reached by river. I only achieved this once when I was invited out by one Gordon Millington, who was an excellent canoeist and hired out a canoe from Benson for the purpose. It was a wonderful experience to glide through the clear, willow-shaded water where each bend brought another lovely vista with the *piece de resistance* the stretch leading to the old bridge at Clifton Hampden and the thatched Barley Mow inn beside it.

Margaret and I once ended up in Burford — we must have hitched for I doubt if we would have cycled that far — and, greatly daring, went into a pub for sandwiches and cider much to the surprise of the locals. We felt very emancipated.

It was at Benson that I resumed my "riding career", begun so disastrously on Marjorie Dovey's pony years before. A charming chap called Vic — we met in Benson canteen — and I heard about a farm in the village of Britwell Salome, not far from Benson, where ponies could be hired out. We cycled out to investigate and were soon mounted on two plump little ponies and went off meandering across the fields on our own. We soon became rather bored by this and urged out steeds to increase their pace. Little enthusiasm was shown until we turned their heads for home when it became a question of hanging on for dear life and praying for survival. Miraculously, we were still in the saddle when we reached the farm and decided, as a result, that we were natural horsemen! Certainly, we went regularly after that, and I have fond memories of autumn landscapes and fields of golden stubble across which Vic and I would gallop with gay abandon. We learned later that this shouldn't have happened as the sharp stalks could have penetrated the tender part of the ponies' feet, and we — and they! — were lucky.

But autumn gave way to an icy winter. Compared with the 8th army, now moving steadily up through Italy, the privations of our lives must have been negligible but, of course, we didn't see it that way. Our biggest problem was heating our billets. Admittedly, there was a coal ration at the beginning of every month and for two, possibly three, days the range in the kitchen would be lit, hot water would gush from our taps and every little grate would glow in the most welcoming fashion. But after that, the coal supply was finished, and it was a case of every WAAF for herself.

We had various sources; one was an adjacent, RAF barrack block. This also had its monthly quota of coal, but it was used to fire the boiler, which would have provided a much more economical method of heating. Certainly, their pile always seemed to last considerably longer than ours. Night-time forays were organized, when we would creep out, armed with sacks and buckets and return, black but triumphant. Of course, we were discovered in the end — it was actually Margaret and her roommate, Gladys who were caught — and the practice became increasingly risky. But that didn't stop Margaret and Gladys. Whenever they went to the Mess from their billet, they had to pass the pile of coal. One of them would always drop something — maybe a knife or fork or a letter or a handkerchief — and, naturally, bend to pick it up. When an upright position had been regained, they would be clutching whatever it was they had dropped plus a lump of coal which they would immediately transfer to their greatcoat pockets. It didn't do their greatcoats much good, but it certainly improved their chances of keeping warm that night!

But by far the most popular method of keeping warm was to smuggle a little electric ring into our rooms and run it off a light fitting. They were strictly verboten as not only was it an enormous fire hazard but seriously overloaded the station's supply of electricity. So periodically our billets would be "raided" by a

WAAF officer whose duty it was to confiscate any illegal electrical appliances. If we heard that she was doing the rounds, rings would be hastily disconnected and pushed under the bed. The resulting smell of singeing mattress must have been a great give-away when she did arrive but was always diplomatically ignored. I think the officers were almost as sorry as we were when we were caught red-handed and one was discovered actually being used. She could then do no other than impound it. It could be collected, we were told, when the owner next went on leave and could take it home with her. Needless to say, they were always collected but never reached home!

I was the proud owner of a stone hot water bottle which, for some reason, I called Humphrey. Even if Humphrey was kicked out of bed in the middle of the night, he was still warm in the morning, and I regularly washed in his contents. Monty had declared that one pint of water per man was sufficient for the daily needs of the 8th army — and I didn't have to shave!

In the outside world, the war continued to progress in our favour and in January, 1943, after months of siege, the Germans surrendered at Stalingrad, the freezing Russian winter having proved too much for them. At home, Winston Churchill decreed that, since the threat of invasion had now been lifted, church bells could be rung again — a very joyous decision and a great boost to our morale. No-one relaxed their determination to win the war as quickly as possible, but people now began to sleep more easily in their beds at night; not, of course, that any of us "bright, young things" had ever had any problem in that direction!

Bill's death was given a certain grim justification when the Germans were finally driven out of North Africa. My mother received a letter from Stan Jones — alias "Guffin" — one of Bill's closest school friends who was in the British 1st army which had reached Tunis through Algeria. He had been greatly looking forward to meeting up with Bill there as the 1st and 8th armies met. It was a most poignant letter but one which my mother was very pleased to receive.

To the distress of many women — and, probably, many men — like my Post Office friend, Joan, and myself, one of our peacetime heroes of the Silver Screen, Leslie Howard, was killed when the civil aircraft on which he was returning from Spain, was shot down by the Germans over the Bay of Biscay. He had been giving lectures to try and persuade the neutral Spaniards to show British war films, which they had agreed to do. He was a typical English "gent", and we loved him.

CHAPTER
TEN

Wartime was a great leveler of social classes. Admittedly, other ranks weren't supposed to mix with commissioned ranks but sometimes it was unavoidable, especially if you were working together. And everyone, no matter what their status in Civvy Street, was much more relaxed with each other — we were, after all, in it together. The same bomb could kill a duke as well as a dustman.

Even so, when I'd been invited to stay overnight at Cherry Trees on one occasion, I was more than a little disconcerted to discover that Air Commodore Boothman — Air Officer Commanding 106 Group — and his wife were coming to dinner. I immediately suggested that I cycle back to camp, but the Macs wouldn't hear of it.

However, matters were considerably improved when their son — a flight lieutenant pilot — arrived with them. He turned out to be a very charming, unassuming sort of guy who probably found it embarrassing to have an AOC for a father. Once dinner was over — a rather subdued affair as far as I was concerned since I felt it safer to speak only when spoken to, rather like dining with the King! — we both escaped into the garden (it was summer time) and had a normal, relaxed conversation. I remember feeling sorry that he wasn't stationed a little nearer to Benson. I can't now remember if he was in Fighter or Bomber Command, but whichever it was, we were devastated when we heard, a few weeks later, that he had been killed.

On another occasion when I was staying there, I met "Woody" who was a flight lieutenant in the Australian Air Force and, if I remember correctly, a navigator. He was waiting to go to Buckingham Palace whence he'd been summoned to receive a DFC. He'd taken part in the raid on the Mohne and Eder Dams when special "bouncing bombs" were dropped from specially adapted Lancaster bombers to breach their walls. It was an incredibly difficult operation involving great accuracy and, of course, great courage. As a result of the operation, a flood tide had swept through Germany's industrial heartland causing enormous damage. The Lancasters of 617 Squadron led by Wing Commander Guy Gibson had been forced to fly perilously low to reach their target, and Woody deemed himself lucky to be alive.

He gave me the awesome responsibility of pressing his uniform before meeting the King, and I can see his jacket now, spread out on Mrs Mac's kitchen table with me standing over it, iron poised and terrified of scorching it. But all went well, and he went off in a Staff car looking very handsome. He was the first Australian I had met, and I was completely disarmed by his easy friendliness.

In the entrance hall of our mess, there were enormous "blow-ups" of the aerial photographs of the Dams that "our" pilots had taken before and after treatment. After meeting Woody, I gazed at them with renewed respect.

Occasionally, an aircraft from Bomber Command would land on our runway, diverted from its home airfield for one reason or another. The differences in the behaviour of their crews compared with our own were quite shocking. There would always be several of them wandering around together, usually with hands in pockets and often tunics unbuttoned and caps off if they preferred it that way. They even, on occasion, whistled after a WAAF if she took their fancy! I once saw a crew commit the most heinous sin of all — strolling across the parade ground in broad daylight while the RAF standard was flying! Benson personnel would have been hung, drawn and quartered if they'd been discovered doing that — well, put on a charge, at least!

On one occasion when we heard that a bomber had landed, I had the most delightful surprise. I was on watch at the time and looked up to see one of the "brown jobs" I had known when I first started work at the Post Office, strolling through the doorway and grinning like a drain.

He and his crew were staying overnight at Benson (I can't now remember why they hadn't made it back to their own station), and we went out that evening. I didn't quite know what to do with him as neither of us drank much, and I couldn't take him to the canteen as he was commissioned. For the same reason, I couldn't exactly parade him around camp, so I took him for a walk — something we had both enjoyed in the old days — through Ewelme village, past the watercress beds and the ancient alms houses and up on to the lower slopes of the Chilterns. Needless to say, we talked our heads off. He was getting married in a few days time to a post office friend of mine, and we toasted the bride-to-be in half pints of cider at a quiet little pub in Ewelme on the way back to camp. It was a happy little interlude, and I'm pleased to report that he survived the war and had a long and happy marriage.

The watercress beds at Ewelme were quite famous and not, as far as Benson was concerned, entirely for their produce. The story went that a group of officers, one of whom was a recent arrival at the camp, had spent the evening in a pub in Ewelme. Returning, rather tipsy, to camp in the dark, the new arrival decided to take a shortcut back to camp across the "fields". Presumably watched by his more informed colleagues, he climbed a gate only to find himself knee-deep in very cold water in a sea of watercress; cue howls of laughter from his new-found "friends" and, no doubt, a few choice expletives from him!

Another watery tale concerned me and the River Thames. I had never learned to swim. The only place to learn in Abergavenny had been in the River Usk where it flowed through Castle Meadows. It was an accepted bathing area with a large wooden hut on stilts (the river sometimes flooded) which contained changing cubicles for men and women. Steps had been constructed where the river was deep (about six feet) and where the river was shallow (about three feet), with a diving board at the deep end. If you wanted to learn to swim, you were placed in a sort of harness which was suspended by a rope from a long, wooden pole, rather like a clothes prop, which was held by Mr Edwards, the gentleman in charge. You were then lowered into the icy depths of the deep end while Mr Edwards walked along the bank, keeping up with the current which could be quite strong, at the same time exhorting you to kick your legs and stretch out your arms. Eventually, when you were deemed proficient enough to stay afloat on your own, you would be released from the harness and allowed to swim unaided under Mr Edwards' watchful eye.

The system worked well for my brother, but I was far too shy to brave such exposure. Admittedly, since the only time my father could take us was six o'clock in the morning, before he went to work, there was never a huge audience, but I could never bring myself to endure it.

Consequently, after my father had paid Mr Edwards the obligatory two pence to give me the privacy of a cubicle in which to change into my hand-knitted swimsuit which, in itself, was a hazard, I would just go down to the shallow end, hold on to the steps and kick my legs. The only time when I combined both arm and leg movements was when my father swam down from the deep end and held my chin while I thrashed around. Needless to say, I never became completely self-propelling.

After I'd left school and we'd moved to Swansea, I had the benefit of the sea and the lovely beaches of the Gower Coast. Salt water, of course, was far more buoyant than the river, and I did occasionally manage a few strokes, but it rarely all came together, and I was always terrified of getting out of my depth.

However, at Benson, it was the custom for off-duty Signal personnel to cycle down to "Benson Plage", as we called it, and swim in the Thames. One day, Margaret — who was an excellent swimmer — and I started off by just sun bathing on the bank of the river but were soon joined by friends who assured me that the best way to learn to swim was simply to jump in at the deep end.

"You'll soon swim then," they assured me.

Looking back, I am amazed at my stupidity, but, ever the optimist, and perhaps afraid of showing my lack of nerve, I did as they said. I walked to the end of the diving board and jumped in!

To this day, I can still see the vivid emerald green of the water as I sank like a stone. When I came up, I was gasping for breath and flailing the water, terrified out of my wits. It was Margaret, who had followed me in and now managed to grab me and somehow tow me to the bank who, I am still convinced, saved my life. The result, of course, was that I became even more terrified of the water than ever.

Thereafter, I restricted myself to sunbathing on the bank. I once dropped off to sleep while I was doing this — I'd just come off night watch — and woke up to find myself dreadfully burned. The next few days were agony while the blisters formed and burst. I could hardly sit down — essential for operating a teleprinter! — but couldn't go on sick parade to be given a soothing lotion or ointment because allowing yourself to become as burned as I had was considered to be a self-inflicted injury and therefore punishable with a charge. I once fell off a horse when it was galloping at a fair lick, thereby badly bruising my back and had to endure the pain for the same reason.

Mind you, our medical officer was Squadron Leader Hussey who was considered a very "good egg" and famous for having accompanied Shackleton on his last Antarctic expedition. Apparently, he had entertained the company with his excellent guitar playing and did, on occasion, perform at Benson, although I never had the pleasure of hearing him. Probably, he would just have cautioned me and given me something for the pain.

Before I leave the river, as it were, there is one other cautionary tale I can tell. There was a certain Warrant Officer Postlethwaite who was particularly unpopular with his staff. But he did possess rather a beautiful body — and he knew it. He liked to hire out a canoe, paddle it to the opposite bank and there strip off his uniform to reveal a magnificent torso clad only in the briefest of swimming trunks. His uniform would be neatly folded and placed in the bottom of the canoe. He would then paddle ostentatiously up and down the river, muscles rippling in the sunshine. But he was never seen to actually go in!

On this particular afternoon — a very hot one — he had tied up on the opposite bank, stripped off as usual but then stretched out on the bottom of the canoe, presumably to top up his tan — no disciplinary action there! Unfortunately for him, several of his staff were taking a swim at the same time and one of them just happened to be an exceptionally good underwater swimmer. You can, perhaps, guess the rest!

Suddenly, there came the most enormous splash and we all sat up — to see the canoe upside down, various pieces of uniform floating away on the current and Warrant Officer Postlethwaite flailing the water rather as I had done.

Naturally, his men went to his rescue with the underwater swimmer diving repeatedly in search of Warrant Officer Postlethwaite's waterlogged shoes and, eventually, Warrant Officer Postlethwaite himself, who was by now in danger of sinking for the third and final time. Everyone, of course, was loud in their expressions of sympathy and puzzlement as to how it could have happened. Warrant Officer Postlethwaite must have had his own theories but could never have proved them.

How he got back to camp in his watery, semi-nude state we never knew. Perhaps he rang up for transport. But we never saw him down at Benson Plage again and, in fact, heard that he was posted soon afterwards.

You would have thought that after blistering so badly, I would have learned my lesson, but not a bit of it. In those days, little was known about the long-term effects of too much exposure to the sun, and to acquire a tan was one of our chief aims in life.

So, on a day-off when everyone was doing other things, I mounted George and pedalled off to the nearby Chilterns, hid George behind a bush and walked up through the trees to a favourite spot where I could stretch out and gaze over the fields to the opposite hillside, or read the book I'd brought with me. Once settled, I took off my jacket and collar and tie, quickly followed by my shoes and stockings.

For a blissful half hour, all was well, and I was almost dozing off when, to my utter astonishment — and theirs! — a detachment of American soldiers suddenly appeared over the immediate horizon and bore down upon me. I couldn't have been more astonished if they'd been a bevy of little green men from Mars.

With astonishing speed, I found myself surrounded by a group of grinning Yanks who sat themselves down around me and proceeded to bombard me with questions. There was a sergeant in their midst who immediately declared a break and everyone pulled out packs of Camels and Lucky Strikes and were soon puffing away. Apparently, they were on some sort of cross-country manoeuvres and coming across a WAAF en deshabille, so to speak, hadn't been one of the landmarks they'd been instructed to watch out for!

They all came from the Deep South, so boasting the lovely drawls, and I soon relaxed and began to enjoy their company, until I happened to glance down at my watch and realised I would have to be getting back to camp. I was on watch at 1700 hours and, clearly, would have to be properly dressed. How was I going to manage this and still observe some degree of propriety?

Should I simply stand up, pick up my shoes and stockings and say, nonchalantly, "Excuse me, guys. I've just got to go and put these on" and head for the nearest bush or should I just scoop everything up in my arms and simply walk away? Easier, perhaps, but a little tough on my bare feet.

The problem was solved for me by the sergeant who had probably decided, anyway, that it was time they all got on with winning the war.

"Come on, fellers," he said, getting to his feet. "Say goodbye to the lovely lady, and we'll be on our way."

And off they went, climbing back over the hill from whence they'd come. Breathing a sigh of relief, I began to pull on my stockings. And then — I could hardly believe it — I saw half a dozen "white flashes" heading up the hill towards me! I can't remember how many times I had sat on that same spot and never seen a sign of life except for the birds and the bees and the butterflies. And now, suddenly, it was practically the hub of the universe!

I watched them coming with mixed feelings. Since the first contingent had arrived on camp and then departed with such heart-fluttering reactions, several more had come and gone and we had grown almost blasé about them. However, it was always good to make new acquaintances. On the other hand, duty called and I still only had on one stocking.

They arrived, like the Americans, with broad grins splitting their faces. They, too, were out on some sort of manoeuvres along the valley and had looked up and seen me, marooned, as it were, in a sea of Americans.

103

Was I, apparently a lone, solitary little Waafie, being intimidated by our "friends" from across the pond? The RAF wasn't as enamoured by the Americans as we were, seeing them, quite rightly, as a challenge on several fronts; more money, better-fitting uniforms and more ways to a girl's heart like a seemingly endless supply of nylons, Hershey bars and, in my case at least, fruit salad.

So they had decided to walk up and investigate. Even when they had seen the Yanks leave, they had carried on, their curiosity, no doubt, aroused.

Strangely enough, I had no hang-ups about explaining my difficulty to them. I suppose I considered them to be familiar territory, while the Yanks were still, in many ways, an unknown quantity.

Once I had explained the situation, they all sat down in a row with their backs to me in the most gentlemanly fashion while I made myself respectable. Once I was fully clothed, I picked up my book and, rather regretfully since one of them seemed exceedingly pleasant, I said goodbye and went back the way I had come, picked up George and cycled back to camp. The afternoon hadn't turned out as I had intended but had still proved not only enjoyable but most instructive. Clearly, if you wanted to meet a feller, the best way to do it was to lie, bare-legged, on a remote hillside on a summer afternoon!

CHAPTER
ELEVEN

Naturally, more of our time was spent on duty in the Section than anywhere else. If there had been a lot of flying, lengthy signals would be brought down from Intelligence — situated on the first floor of SHQ — giving detailed information of what the aerial photographs had revealed. These had to be transmitted to other Groups and stations, and this was done through a broadcast system set up through our own little switchboard, using a series of plugs. It sometimes happened that an operator would get to the end of a very long and intricate signal and then, when the switchboard operator went through the system, asking each station to give confirmation of receipt, it would be discovered that, for some technical reason beyond her control, someone hadn't received it. For a couple of minutes, the air would be blue while the sender of the signal let off steam, for the whole signal would now have to be sent again. This always seemed to be the case when Squadron Leader Ellis strolled in to see how we were faring. Suffering — as we were to discover later! — with having had a very strict upbringing and taught somewhat conventional ideas upon how nicely brought-up females should react to such a contingency, he would flinch slightly and beat a hasty retreat but would always maintain a sympathetic silence.

Although SHQ Signals was staffed almost entirely by WAAF, we did occasionally acquire RAF personnel. Two of these were Reg and Arthur who had just endured a tour of duty on a remote Scottish island in the Hebrides where most of the native population had been of the four-legged, woolly variety. To them, Benson was like a four-star, luxury hotel. Reg was soon joined by his wife, Kay — also a teleprinter op. whom he had met and married on a previous station — and they lived out in the village, the envy of us all.

Arthur's wife was a civilian who lived in Buckinghamshire but who would frequently come to stay in the Riverside Café when Arthur could get permission to join her. He was slightly older than the rest of us and was a professional church organist and choir master in Civvy Street. He lived for music and sometimes, when we were quiet, he would pretend that his teleprinter was an organ, pull out imaginary stops and let his fingers "wander idly over the ivory keys", at the same time throwing back his head and mouthing the words of a hymn or oratorio. At other times, you'd catch him gazing vacantly into space, his mouth slightly ajar, his arms beating the air like a frenetic bookmaker, and you'd know he was simply conducting an imaginary choir. Not, as Squadron Leader Ellis obviously thought when he caught him at it one day, having a mental breakdown. As I remember it, they just gazed at each other in mutual embarrassment, until Arthur explained what he was up to. They then had a

106

most interesting talk about music in general and choral work in particular.

We were all very fond of Arthur, so you can imagine my delight when, many years later, uniforms long since discarded, I discovered him to be the church organist-cum-choir master in the parish church of the little market town of Winslow, where I had just moved to.

One of our regular diversions when on morning watch, and not too busy, was to "send out to Mrs Crane's". Mrs Crane was an enterprising, middle-aged lady who lived just outside the camp gates and made a living by baking exquisite pies and cakes and selling them to the likes of us. Besides being an excellent cook, she was also a very jolly lady whom it was always a pleasure to chat to. I was quite often the one who was sent on these errands as George boasted a capacious basket on his handlebars in which the goodies could be safely stowed.

One of the advantages of working in SHQ was having a plentiful supply of hot water on tap in the communal ablutions. As well as Signal Section, the station commander, the WAAF "Queen Bee" and Intelligence, mostly staffed by officers, had their offices there. All these illustrious creatures would have expected hot water. And since they could hardly forbid access to us lesser mortals, we made as much use of it as we could. So, if night duties weren't busy, we would rinse out our smalls and hang them on the radiators to dry or bring towels and shampoo and wash our hair in the toilet washbasins.

And then, to our huge delight, a WAAF hairdresser appeared in our midst. For the princely sum of sixpence — 5p in present day currency — we could have a shampoo and set. We also had the benefit of a camp laundry and a camp tailor. If any of our clothes wore out, they were replaced without question once they had been officially "condemned". All in all, we were looked after very well. Our food, even if sometimes stodgy and unappetising was served up to us three times a day without fail. And for those who got up for it, there was an egg for breakfast on Sunday mornings. We never had to lift a finger to shop for it or cook it. Not for us the mundane necessity of queuing at the butchers or dropping everything because you suddenly heard on the grapevine that he had sausages.

Admittedly, there was a weekly institution known as "Domestic Night" — usually Tuesdays — when all WAAF were confined to camp for the evening for the express purpose of cleaning their billets, polishing their buttons and mending their clothes, if required. And talking of clothes, the airmen always maintained that we'd stolen their pyjamas! Apparently, before war broke out, airmen were issued with pyjamas; blue and white striped, winciette pyjamas. But once hostilities were declared, and the WAAF became an accepted part of the Service, the issue was transferred to the airwomen and the airmen, not being issued with sheets either — although I don't think this was anything to do with us — had to go to bed with nothing but the "rough, male kiss of blankets" caressing their limbs. And while

Rupert Brooke might not have minded, they certainly did!

After Margaret and I had been at Benson for just over a year, a camp cinema was opened. It may have been improvised from a spare hangar, but it had all the requisites of a proper cinema with a good-sized screen, rows of tip-up seats and a stage. The stage was particularly important because we occasionally had live theatre. I particularly remember a performance of Terence Rattigan's *While The Sun Shines* straight from the West End. Whatever the show and wherever you sat, it only cost sixpence a time.

"Going to the flicks" on an RAF camp was like no similar outing in Civvy Street. Airmen, no doubt like all servicemen, were quick to read a double meaning into the most innocent of remarks. While at first I had no idea what all the raucous laughter was about, I was soon enlightened by more worldly friends and would indulge in a surreptitious giggle or two, myself, even though part of my convent-bred psyche was more than a little shocked.

Looking back, I can't remember that I read many books, other than the Book Club choices my mother would send on to me every month, but I did place a regular order for the *Spectator* with the newsagent who used to sell his wares in the mess every day. I would read it studiously from cover to cover even though a lot of it was way above my head.

I suppose that much of our spare time was spent in writing letters — mail was a great source of comfort. And we did sew and knit. Since all our clothes were provided for us, our clothing coupons disappeared and while we obviously had to toe the line as far as our outer garments were concerned, what we wore underneath was our own business — provided, of course, that it didn't show.

Parachute silk, remnants of which would sometimes have to be officially discarded, were at a premium. If the pieces were large enough, abbreviated nighties and, of course, knickers could be made and, on one occasion, even a wedding dress.

Kit inspections were held from time to time when all our kit had to be laid out on our beds, ready for inspection by an officer. It never mattered if you'd lost or mislaid something as the standard answer to any query would be — "one on, ma'am, one on the bed and one in the wash." I don't suppose the officers enjoyed the procedure any more than we did, and I'm quite sure they never bothered to check if we were telling the truth.

Like several of my friends, I knitted a sweater out of darning wool; an elaborate process involving the tying together of strands of wool and then knitting them up so that the knots, if you were lucky, didn't show. It was best to use several different colours, thus producing a marled effect so that the knots, if they did appear, would then be less obtrusive. I remember choosing dark green, maroon and pale grey and being very pleased with the result.

I had one very useful piece of sartorial good fortune. A friend of Mrs Mac's had contacts in the States and had been sent several pairs of nylon stockings.

Eventually, these would ladder or be snagged but not, as would be the case these days, immediately discarded. They would be passed on to those friends who were particularly skilled with a needle. Such a one was Mrs Mac. And she, being of a generous nature, passed several pairs on to me. I can still remember the feeling of blissful luxury when I wore them on leave, darns or no darns. Glamorous didn't even begin to describe it!

Everyone, service personnel and civilians alike, became skilled at using whatever material was available for their purpose. My mother even knitted a stair carpet out of string using the same method that I had used for my sweater, cutting the string into identical lengths that were then tied together and knitted up on very thick, wooden needles; the only difference being that for a carpet the knots had to be visible, thus forming a creditable "pile" that looked quite attractive.

Mrs Mac made several rag rugs, using remnants from any old garment or pieces of material she had, the brighter the better. Although they were great dustgatherers, they looked extremely effective, especially in an old cottage like Cherry Trees.

Nothing was wasted. Neighbouring pigs must have grown fat on the pig swill they were fed; anything left on our plates after a meal being conscientiously scraped off into a pig swill bin.

And to this day, I always cut open my toothpaste tubes so that the last smear can be extracted. It's the same with soap; the last sliver of the old bar being stuck on to the new. Younger friends think I'm parsimonious but my contemporaries know better!

CHAPTER
TWELVE

No-one was more surprised than I when I was made up to corporal. Not only surprised but alarmed. I had absolutely no wish to tell other people what to do; nor to maintain the standard of behaviour expected of my exalted status. No more pinching of coal or squeezing through the gap in the perimeter fence after hours, no more riding back from the village without a rear light.

Because I would now be automatically in charge of a watch, I rehearsed an elaborate scenario whereby I would start doing a job and then say casually to one of the other watch members, "Just finish this for me, would you please Daisy — or Mary — or Angie . . .".

Of course, I was worrying over nothing. Nobody ever waited to be asked, they just got on with whatever was waiting to be done, only bringing me in when there was a problem, which I was quite happy either to solve or to take to a higher authority.

With an inward sigh of relief, I started to enjoy the few perks that came with the job. To begin with, I stayed in the same married quarter but moved into the back bedroom, which I shared with another corporal, Pat Crocker. We soon became great friends. She was an RT op with sparks on her sleeve — I envied her those

— and worked at an outpost somewhere in the surrounding countryside. For this, she wore battledress, which consisted of trousers and a blouse-effect top — which I also envied — and she was very pretty. Not surprisingly, she was engaged — to a corporal radio mechanic called Des.

We had a fireplace in our little room, but it was much smaller than the others so was that much easier to fill. As Pat was working out in the country, she could go on regular "wooding" or pine-cone collecting expeditions, and our room always seemed to be warm and cosy in the winter time. She would also bring back any left-over food from the rations that the out-station was allowed. My standard of living improved dramatically.

And then I was moved, temporarily, to our satellite station at Mount Farm. Situated beyond Dorchester, it was that much nearer to Oxford, so that my visits there became even more frequent.

It had a tiny teleprinter cabin with just one machine and a bed, and we were never very busy. Night duties were usually slept through, uninterrupted. It was altogether more casual than Benson, and "callers" were frequently entertained with cups of tea through the window that opened straight out on to the airfield. I became quite friendly with a flight sergeant pilot through this means. When he knew I was on duty, he would come and tap on the window — rather like a robin asking to be fed! We went to several Mount Farm dances, and my dancing skills improved no end. Afterwards, we would take a somewhat circuitous route back to WAAF quarters through the surrounding hay fields!

And then the Americans took over and life, you could say, was never quite the same again. P38s or Lightnings — they had a double fuselage rather like an airborne catamaran — flew in, and Spits and Mossies flew out. Sadly, I packed up my kit and went back to Benson.

As time went by, the Americans proved to be good fun. Parties, to which we were invited, were held where food was plentiful. I particularly remember the dishes of exotic fruit salad — something we hadn't seen since hostilities began. Nylons were also dispensed to the favoured few, but none ever came my way.

I remember being chatted up by one Yank in the Bullcroft canteen who strolled over to my table where I was sitting alone and produced what I later discovered to be one of the oldest chat-up lines in the book but, in my naïve ignorance, I accepted at face value.

"Say, do you have a sister?"

"No, I'm afraid not."

But by then, he was sitting opposite me and solemnly shaking his head. "You're right. There couldn't be two girls as cute as you!"

I was entranced, I had just indulged in a new hair style called the Liberty Cut where the hair was cut to a length of two and a half inches all over and then, if necessary as it was in my case, permed. The result was a head of tight little curls, and I had thought the style suited me. Here was confirmation that I was right!

It was probably just as well that I was on evening watch that day, but by the time I left him, we had arranged to meet on the following evening; on the river bank under a certain tree. Very romantic! It was, I hasten to add, summer time and therefore light until quite late.

I was convinced he wouldn't turn up — in spite of the Liberty Cut — so, as a precaution, I arrived armed with a book. But he did turn up and was quite convinced I'd brought it in case I was bored with his company. However, we sorted it out, and he actually ruled my behaviour to be "kinda cute"!

I remember nothing at all of what we did afterwards, but I never saw him again and was left with a vague memory of what I later identified to myself as the American Male Smell — a combination of aftershave and whisky. Aftershave hadn't yet reached the chin of the average British serviceman and whisky was an almost non-existant luxury, so it was a peculiarly distinctive and not unpleasant smell.

I only had one other "close" encounter with a Yank — and it was very sad.

I'd gone on a blind date with a very glamorous, blonde WAAF whom I didn't know very well. She had a date with an American pilot at Mount Farm who had a friend who wanted to meet an English girl. Would I oblige? Ever ready for new experiences and with the ever-present thought of tins of fruit salad, I went.

It was an unmitigated disaster. We were to meet them on the officers' mess at Mount Farm where we had a couple of drinks. We then split up, and before I realised what was happening, I found myself alone with him in his room. Sadly, I spent the next twenty minutes assuring him that I had absolutely no wish to go to bed with him. To his credit, he then gave up but clearly had no further wish for my company. Sex was the only reason I'd been invited.

The sad part is that the next day he was killed when his P38 was shot down somewhere over Germany. For weeks, I felt guilty and somehow responsible. Would he have been more relaxed and therefore more aware of what was happening, had I "given in" or would I, as Pat was quick to point out when I told her all about it, be counting the days before my next period?

I had one very beautiful, blonde friend called Sandra who found she was pregnant after her pilot fiancé was killed. In those days, having an illegitimate baby was almost on a par with killing your grandmother or taking a pot shot at the King, so we were all very worried about her. However, fortunately for Sandra, her fiancé's parents were so devastated at their loss, they welcomed the opportunity of helping to bring up their son's child.

Moral standards must have changed during the war, but for girls like me with no knowledge of birth control and only the scantiest understanding of how babies were conceived in the first place — my mother never told me a thing and, naturally, it wasn't a subject the nuns had brought up at school! — they remained rigid. "So far and no further", and the chaps, on the whole, accepted it. Or, at least, the ones I met did. But looking back, I'm surprised I never found myself in an ugly situation. "So far and no further" must have been an almost impossible rule for some red-blooded males to abide by.

I know that many civilians had the idea that girls in the Services did little but pop in and out of bed with their male counterparts, but it simply wasn't true. Of course, it happened sometimes, but on the whole we carried on as if we were still living at home, as most of us were before we joined up.

CHAPTER
THIRTEEN

Pat and I knew about D-Day at least twenty-four hours before it happened. She, because Des had gone, and I because I'd transmitted the signal giving other stations in our Group the full details of what would be happening, where and when.

Cycling around the perimeter en route to the canteen that evening, we met the ops controller who'd given me the signal for transmission. Hopping off his bike, he reminded us of the importance of keeping our mouths shut. Solemnly, we assured him that we wouldn't have dreamt of doing anything else.

In fact, we'd had our suspicions for several weeks since coming back from the village at night had often entailed pressing ourselves into the hedgerow to allow convoys of dimly-lit army vehicles to pass on their way south. And then, a couple of days before D-Day, some of our aircraft had been printed with broad black and white stripes around their fuselages,

When I came back from night duty next morning, Pat had the wireless on with news more or less straight from the beaches. It was very worrying for Pat until she started getting letters from Des, but for those of us who hadn't anyone out there, it was a time of great optimism. At last the end was in sight, and Pat began making plans for her wedding when Des managed to get home on leave.

I, to my astonishment, was sent on an NCO's course to Gosport, near Portsmouth. A little late in the day, I thought, for I'd been a corporal for almost a year, but it was all experience, and I'd never been to that particular neck of the woods.

The Orderly Room routed me via Paddington and Waterloo (no problem there these days for I'd spent several weekends in London with my father) and was crossing the concourse at Waterloo when my gas cape — neatly rolled in the nape of my neck — suddenly started to cascade down my back. My gas cape, I should explain, had always had a mind of its own. It was supposed to be rolled and tied in such a way that it would unroll immediately if the white tape that was dangling over my shoulder was pulled. This never worked. When required to, as on a gas exercise, it would remain obstinately and embarrassingly in situ. No amount of tugging had the slightest effect. Now, in the middle of a very busy Waterloo station, it decided to take to the air. Down it came, billowing around my shoulders and making me look like the Angel Gabriel in camouflage gear. Short of putting down my respirator and suitcase and spreading the cape out on the ground, going down on my knees and re-rolling it, I could do nothing except billow on my way, trying to ignore the broad grins of station staff and fellow travellers. It wasn't until I reached the sanctuary of the Portsmouth train which, luckily for me was already waiting, and had found an empty compartment, that I could do anything about it. But the incident set the tone for the course that followed; more embarrassment but with distinctly comic overtones.

There were probably about thirty of us, and we lived — as seemed my fate — in married quarters with six of us to a house. Naturally, we all chummed up immediately, but it was a girl called Bobby Rowbotham whom I remember particularly.

On the whole, the course proved to be interesting and also good fun. The fun aspect was largely due to the section officer in charge of us — a very pretty young woman with a great sense of humour who treated us like human beings instead of numbers on a payroll. The sergeant, with whom we had more frequent contact, belonged to the old school. This was never more evident than when we were on parade and learning how to drill a squad. Or not, as the case might be! It was a nightmare I had been dreading.

I had a naturally quiet voice that even the person sitting next to me would sometimes find difficult to hear. In school plays, I had always been accused of "eating my words" and not opening my mouth. Now, I was expected to shout commands at a squad of women drawn up on a windy parade ground with a flock of seagulls squawking away above their heads.

Each of us had to take our turn at being "Corporal of the Day". This meant marshalling the other girls into a squad outside our billets first thing in the morning — with the sergeant in attendance, of course — and marching them to breakfast and everywhere else during the course of the day and this, of course included the parade ground where they would have to be put through their paces. Right from the start, we were told that whatever command was given, even if it was clearly the wrong one, it must be obeyed. So that, on the day when I was duty corporal and had marched the squad down to the mess for breakfast, halted them, then given the command "Left Turn", they all immediately turned their backs on me. Clearly, the command should have been, "Right Turn"!

Apart from a sharp intake of breath from the sergeant who had shadowed us throughout and was now lurking at my elbow, there was complete silence. Repressing an hysterical urge to giggle, I collected my very scattered wits and gave the command to "Turn About". As one, they turned, poker-faced, and to my enormous relief, faced towards me.

"At least," murmured the Sergeant in my ear, after I had dismissed them, "You kept your head."

Such, however, was not the case on the parade ground that afternoon.

I did manage to get them there in one piece as it were. But the afternoon was a debacle. I cannot now remember the sequence of commands I gave them or, indeed, what those commands were. All I can now remember — and will until my dying day — is the result; half the squad marching smartly due north and the other, equally as smartly, due south with "me and my shadow" in an ever-increasing space between. Panic-stricken, I gazed after the rapidly disappearing halves of my squad.

"Say something," suggested my shadow blandly. "If it's only goodbye!"

Eventually, before both halves disappeared completely, one up the NAAFI steps, the other out to sea, the sergeant, with a voice like a foghorn brought them, miraculously, together again and entrusted them once more to my tender care. No doubt, she'd seen it all before. There was much laughter when, at the end of the day, I dismissed them for the last time, and the Sergeant had disappeared.

However, I did manage to acquire a few Brownie points before the course ended. We each had to give a talk upon any subject of our choice as long as it had some connection with service life. It had to last ten minutes which, we discovered, was quite a long time. I decided to talk about George, my trusty steed, and managed to raise a few laughs in the process. I felt quite chuffed.

I returned to Benson much as I had left it but with a voice that I had, at last, managed to project, so perhaps it did me some good. Not that, to my great relief, I ever had to drill a squad again during the remainder of my service life.

CHAPTER
FOURTEEN

On Des's first leave from Europe, Pat was married at her home, and I was invited as a witness. It was a very happy, informal affair with Pat rushing out of the house on her wedding morning to buy a pair of gloves. In retrospect, I wonder why. She wouldn't have needed them at the altar so they must have been to complete her going-away outfit. Their honeymoon was spent, as Pat had always hoped it would be, in the village of Combe Martin in North Devon.

The other romantic happening at that time was, to say the least, startling although, in the end, highly satisfactory. It was to do with my friend Margaret and Squadron Leader Ellis. Margaret had never formed any permanent liaison with the opposite sex. She dillied and dallied and seemed to get on particularly well with the Americans at Mount Farm. But she had certainly formed no significant relationship with anyone of commissioned rank. Both of us — particularly me! — had thought our junior signals officer, who hailed from the Welsh Valleys, particularly handsome with his black curly hair and very blue eyes and had been very sad when he was posted up to the Shetlands. But we had soon recovered.

Squadron Leader Ellis, on the other hand, had never, as far as we knew, shown any particular interest in any one female. He was a fair-haired, blue-eyed young man with regular features who, until he smiled, had a somewhat diffident air. However, when he did smile, it was like the sun breaking through on a frosty morning. Apart from brief comments when he came into the Section, we didn't have a lot to do with him. We knew he had a Cambridge degree and was "rather brainy", and we considered him to be an "OK guy" but somewhat aloof. But all this was about to change.

One sunny, summer morning, Margaret was called into his office. We were on watch together at the time — we were having one of our "friendly" periods — and I watched her go with some trepidation. What had she been up to? Apart from harbouring an illicit electric ring, as we all did, possibly nicking the odd bit of coal or crawling into camp under the perimeter fence if she didn't know the password of the day — again, something we all did — her conduct, as far as I knew, had been blameless. Was there some dreadful news from home? But if so, it would have been the job of the WAAF admin officer to break it to her.

A good half hour later, she came back to the section, looking as if she'd been pole-axed. "Tell you later!" she hissed out of the corner of her mouth. And she did.

Apparently, William had sat her down and informed her a) that he had been posted to Reykavik, in Iceland, b) that he loved her and had done for some time and c) if neither she nor her parents had any objection, would she consider spending a few days leave with him at his

124

family home while she got to know him better and considered marrying him? No wonder she'd looked pole-axed! None of us — and certainly not her — had had any idea of his feelings for her.

However, as she pointed out, there was nothing to lose, and he was a nice guy. So off they went to his family home for seven days leave — William fixed this up with WAAF Admin! — after which, whatever Margaret's decision, William would be going on to Reykavik. Meanwhile, the rest of Signals — and, indeed, the whole camp by now, for the news spread like wild fire — held its breath.

At the end of the seven days — during which time, my company had never been so sought after as everyone tried to pump me for details — back came Margaret looking suitably dewy-eyed and sporting an enormous diamond solitaire on her engagement finger. Signals let out its collective breath and demanded to know the details.

Apparently, William, still determined to do the honourable thing, had insisted upon sending Margaret back to camp with some emblem, at least, of propriety, hence the ring. If, after weeks of correspondence and another leave, Margaret decided not to marry him, she could easily break off their engagement.

But Margaret didn't, and a few months later, several of us went into Oxford in our "best blues" for their wedding. Off they went on their honeymoon to somewhere in North Devon and Margaret came back as LACW Ellis. After the war, they had a long and happy life together with two lovely daughters — I was godmother to their eldest — and several talented grandchildren to show for it.

Looking back, I have always been impressed by William's integrity. Feeling as he did about Margaret, it must have been hell for the poor chap to see her going out with other men while he sat on the side lines and watched. Protocol, because he was her senior officer, demanded that he could do nothing about it. She was a very pretty girl with a lovely figure, dark hair, pink cheeks and long-lashed, very blue eyes that possessed a "natural eye-liner" — they looked as if they'd been "rubbed in with a sooty finger" as my mother used to say. His posting to Iceland must have been like a gift from the Gods since it meant he could come clean and declare himself. Sometimes, I have wondered if he deliberately applied for the posting.

CHAPTER
FIFTEEN

David was back in England. He had passed out of his pilot's course with flying colours — please forgive the pun! — and was returning home as a fully fledged pilot officer. He would be having leave very soon after disembarking and, naturally, would go home for it. "Home" was a small village in Wiltshire and not that far from Oxford. Could we meet there? And he hoped I wouldn't mind, but he would have a friend with him; a young South African named Geoff who had been on the same course as him and with whom he had become friendly. Geoff knew no-one in Britain so, naturally, David had invited him home for part of his leave. He would be going on to another friend for the rest of it.

I didn't mind at all. In fact, I welcomed it. Now that the long-awaited moment was imminent, I felt suddenly very shy. (David later confessed to the same feeling.) So to balance Geoff, as it were, I decided to invite a fellow WAAF — May O'Shea — to come with me.

May — also a teleprinter op. — was, in several ways, different from the rest of us. To begin with, she was from Southern Ireland, a neutral country, and therefore under no coercion or obligation to join the British Services, but she had done so because she believed the anti-Nazi cause for which Britain was fighting to be a just one. She was older than the rest of us, having reached the advanced age of thirty-five — incredibly ancient when viewed from the perspective of people in their early twenties! — and she was also a devout Catholic. No one else among my friends was particularly religious, although Pat had become a Catholic because Des was one, not that there'd been any pressure from him to convert. She just couldn't bear to be different from him. None of us, besides May, went to church unless we were ordered to do so on a Church Parade when C. of E. personnel would march to the beautiful old church of Ewelme, with its equally as lovely mediaeval alms houses. Signals personnel rarely were on Church Parade since we always had the excuses of "being on night duty", "sleeping after night duty" or just plain "on duty" or "out of camp on a weekend pass". But May was a regular attendee at Sunday Mass, and we always respected her wishes.

Apart from being a good friend, always ready with a sympathetic ear if I wanted to unburden my soul — a rare occasion, but it could happen — May was just the right person to take with me to meet David. By great good fortune, she had friends in Rhodesia and had been kind enough to write to them and tell them about David's presence in their country. Showing typical Rhodesian hospitality, they had immediately contacted him and invited him to stay whenever he had leave and, as a result, he had become a firm friend of the family, so May would now be able to have first hand news of her friends. Probably more sensible than the rest of us and certainly more mature in her outlook, she was, in any case, the perfect person to smooth over any awkwardness between David and myself.

Naturally, there was no convenient bus to get us to Oxford railway station in time to meet David and Geoff at 11a.m. when their train was due, so we hitched. As luck would have it, we had no success for the first half hour, and I began to panic. When an obliging lorry driver eventually drew up, I could have hugged him. However, my delight was short lived. He had crates of live chickens piled in the back and daren't, therefore, go too fast. But at least we were on our way. We climbed up into his cab and tried not to notice other lorries now speeding past us at a rate of knots!

Even now, I can remember the mixed emotions I was experiencing as I sat, practically perched on the gear lever and trying not to glance, too obviously, at my watch. Part of me was full of happy anticipation that we were to meet again, but part of me was highly apprehensive that I should find David changed into someone with whom I now had little in common. After all — and I don't think I've mentioned this before — I was three years older than he. Would he have matured into someone beyond recognition? However, there was one thing for certain — there was no going back now. Nor, deep down, did I want to.

We were only a few minutes late, but the train had been on time and, as we panted up the slight incline towards the station, we could see them waiting outside; two figures — Geoff slightly taller than David — clad in brand-new officers' uniforms, pristine white wings on their chests, pristine white rings around their cuffs — an indication that they had reached the dizzy rank of pilot officer — and looking rather as if they'd be quite at home on top of a Christmas tree!

It was interesting that David later told me that, just as I had thought they looked a shade too neat and clean, he had thought May and I looked a trifle shabby and well-worn. When I thought about it, I could see why he should think that. After all, we had had our uniforms for three years and, although we were both wearing our "best blues", they had been in pretty constant use. Probably the whole of Britain and its occupants was looking pretty shabby by now. Rhodesia must have seemed like Eldorado by comparison. But back to Oxford railway station —

We didn't kiss. In fact, I rather think we shook hands and then formal introductions were made, and I thanked heaven for having brought May with me. Immediately, she plied David with questions about the health and well-being of her friends while I did my best to make Geoff feel at home. An early lunch was suggested, and we all piled into a nearby café where we planned the day.

David had an appointment with his tutor to discuss his future University studies; May had some urgent shopping, and I was given the task of finding a hotel for Geoff where he could spend the night. Apparently, he wanted to spend the next day sightseeing and, I think, also wanted to give David time alone with his family. Afterwards, I realised that it would have been more sensible for me to have simply escorted him to a hotel and stayed outside while he went in to make a reservation, but since David had asked me to organize it, I felt obliged to do it myself. In hindsight, it's clear that, in spite of two years of service life, I had lost little of my convent-bred naïvete; the receptionist of each hotel we tried simply looked us both up and down in a meaningful manner and stated, without even checking, that no rooms were available. They didn't even bother to say they were sorry. After my third attempt, the penny finally dropped — I think Geoff was as naïve as me — and for the fourth attempt he went in on his own and was immediately successful.

When we all eventually met up again, there wasn't a great deal of time left before May and I caught a bus back to Benson — we'd had enough hitching for one day — so we spent it giving Geoff a quick tour of some of the colleges which he could look at more thoroughly the next day. But the main objective had been achieved; David and I had met and had arranged to spend a few days leave together in Swansea.

There, under the benevolent jurisdiction of my mother, who couldn't wait to meet David, we relaxed and got to know each other all over again. The weather was excellent — it was mid-summer by now — and we made several trips down to the Gower peninsula, swaying gently on the top of a double-decker bus. My mother, who had taken to David on sight, packed us up enormous picnics, including the *piece de resistance* hard-boiled eggs, on whose shells she had taken great delight in drawing smiley little faces.

Most of the beaches were still covered with tall, wooden poles — an anti-tank device — but we walked along the cliff tops and ate our sandwiches with only the seagulls for company. It was great.

We met up with several of my Post Office friends and took my mother to the cinema, which she loved. All in all, it was a good leave.

I doubt if I'd changed very much since we'd first met, but David certainly had. For the most part, he was still the same happy-go-lucky young man I'd fallen in love with, but at the same time he'd also acquired more responsibilities. Not only had he learned to fly a complex fighter plane, he'd also become a commissioned officer. The latter, while it gave him a certain gravitas that went with additional responsibilities, also seemed to give him an entrée into a more sophisticated world than mine. Both of us had come from similar, lower middle-class backgrounds, although his father was the headmaster of a village school and far more academic than mine was. Growing up, our standards of living had been much the same. But David was clever and had benefited from living on the doorstep of a small public school from which he had gained a scholarship to Oxford, something my brother Bill had failed to do.

In those days, an Oxbridge education was still the "open sesame" to a more glamorous way of life and many excellent jobs. And while I may have had certain aspirations in that direction — my mother had certainly had them for me! — hadn't acquired the necessary attributes of confidence and personality. Basically, I was still at heart the shy, socially inept little "country girl". Quite happy in a one-to-one situation and sometimes even sparkling in the right company, that is, if I knew people well, but hopeless — and hapless! — in a crowd of self-confident young people. Maybe I had hidden depths, but they took a lot of digging out! Basically, while I'd been very much at home among a crowd of young Airforce cadets, I was less so among the commissioned ranks — except possibly the Canadian variety! However, this didn't become apparent until later and certainly not on that first leave we spent together.

When our leave ended, and I went back to Benson and David to an Advanced Flying Training School — we were still at war with Japan — I was more than happy, and I think David was, too. We hadn't actually discussed the future, but we seemed to have tacitly agreed that we had one.

CHAPTER
SIXTEEN

Suddenly, in Europe at least, it was all over. Early in May, 1945, Field Marshall Montgomery received the surrender of all German forces in North-West Germany, Holland and Denmark. The German army in Italy and Norway had already capitulated. As luck would have it, three of us from Signals were on a train bound for Yatesbury in Wiltshire and a teleprinter course when peace was announced. One of us immediately jumped train, and went back to Benson to celebrate with her boyfriend. Needless to say, no disciplinary action was ever taken.

The surrender of the Japanese came later that year, in August, when release dates were promulgated — I think that was the word they used. Married women, naturally, would go first and that, of course, now included Margaret. August 1946 seemed the most likely date for me, so I settled down to enjoy my last year at Benson. But it wasn't to be. To my great annoyance, I and two other WAAF teleprinter ops were posted to Padgate, near Warrington in Lancashire, a major RAF recruiting centre. You would have thought, I moaned to my flight sergeant when he gave me the news, that Records in Gloucester, having forgotten about me for three years, would have left me in peace for the remaining one. He made strong clucking noises of sympathy, assured me he would be sorry to lose me but that he could do nothing about it.

Looking back, those three years at Benson were good years. Of course there was a war on; of course people were being killed, my own brother among them, but if it had to happen, then Benson was, as far as I was concerned, the best place to be. Until then, apart from a school trip to Stratford to see Donald Wolfit play Hamlet and a trip by the Swansea Ladies Hockey team, of which I was a somewhat indifferent member, to play the London Welsh, I had never been out of Wales. So the war allowed me to discover England, as it were.

Situated as it was on the River Thames, on the edge of the Chilterns and not too far from the Berkshire Downs and the Cotswolds, Benson was a lovely place to be. It's interesting that now in England, Wales is the country I visit regularly and would probably choose to live in, were it not for family commitments. But at the age of twenty, leaving it meant discovering a whole new world and one that I enjoyed to the utmost.

But now it was to be Lancashire; the "industrial North" as far as I was concerned. I left Benson after many fond farewells, particularly to Mr and Mrs Mac at Cherry Trees (I saw them again after the war, but it was never quite the same). But at least I had company as I left Benson on an appropriately rainy day. With me went two bonny Scottish lasses; Kathy McNee and Margaret Sutherland. I remember that it was still raining when we reached Warrington and there was no transport to meet us. No longer the meek little recruit, I rang Padgate from the RTO's office and eventually it came.

Of course, the gloom and doom didn't last; the permanent personnel at Padgate were far too interesting for that. Once peace had been declared, there was little need for aircrew or any of the attendant jobs like flight mechanics and fitters, which had been done by both WAAF and RAF personnel. But redundant people couldn't be released into "Civvy Street" all at the same time and so flood the labour market. So, while they awaited their turn to be demobbed, they had to be found something to do. Thus it became the norm to find non-commissioned aircrew, for instance, working in the Orderly Room alongside people like Heather Grassie from Perth, an ex radar op. She had been posted to Padgate about three weeks before we three had arrived from Benson, and we all met up in a canteen in Warrington where the three Scottish accents acted like magnets. We all became firm friends but sadly, Kathy had to be discharged soon afterwards because of chronic asthma, and Margaret was given a posting nearer home, but Heather and I developed a friendship that was to last for many years.

She was engaged, and soon to be married, to Dennis, another R/T op. still stationed at her old station, somewhere in the Midlands. Our quarters now were in a big Nissan hut rather like the ones at Innsworth where we'd all joined up and our beds were next to each other. The only "personal" area we had was our bed space, a bedside locker and a long locker in which uniforms could be hung. Any other personal possessions had to be crammed into our suitcases which were stowed under the bed. But it didn't matter; it was for a limited period only. Everything was for a limited period only, and so life was much more relaxed; after all, the main reason for our being there in the first place was now over.

As Padgate was a non-operational station, Signals Section consisted only of a teleprinter cabin with, if I remember correctly, two teleprinters, at least two armchairs and a little pot-bellied stove which burned coke. The armchairs were always occupied either by a teleprinter op. waiting for the occasional arrival of a signal or by a casual caller, of which there were many. The existing staff already there when we arrived were Pat Mee, a pretty little brunette who had a disconcerting habit of answering telephone calls with "Mee, here!", Jean Walker, a glamorous blonde who lived in Blackpool and Norman, a serious-minded lad with a nice sense of humour.

The casual callers included Gordon Metcalfe who had a talent for quick but very accurate sketches of his colleagues and Don and Geoff, "retired" pilots, all of whom now worked in the Orderly Room. Many cups of tea were brewed and laced heavily with Carnation Milk from Contented Cows (tinned), and many discussions were enjoyed about what we would do when we were demobbed. I particularly remember one sergeant, whom someone had brought in for a cup of tea, confiding in me that he was going to work with his future father-in-law who had just started producing something called "plastic" which, he assured me, would have a great future. How right he was! Another hopeful, but perhaps one not so assured of so much success, was a young man who intended to be a stand-up comedian and would solemnly record in a little notebook any jokes or "bon mots" we might utter. Sadly, I can't now remember his name, but I'm pretty sure it wasn't Bob Monkhouse or Benny Hill!

Besides drinking tea and nattering our heads off, we also smoked — many of us like chimneys. After all, we were being given so many cigarettes for nothing and so many at a very reduced rate, so it wasn't surprising. Fortunately, I never managed to inhale without choking, so I never really became addicted and eventually gave it up without too much effort. It was more of a social ploy really, giving one hand something to do while the other held a glass or tankard. For it was at Padgate that I also succumbed to the attractions of alcohol!

It was a time for demob parties for someone was always leaving. We would walk to the nearest pub and do our best to make the evening memorable for whoever it was before they set off for their demob centre next day. Because it was the cheapest drink, we all drank beer. My capacity was two pints which I consumed in four half-pints not enough to turn me into an alcoholic but enough to make me extremely cheerful on the way back to camp.

Heather and I were always together on these occasions and often accompanied by Scotty and Harry, two other Orderly Room buddies of hers. One of Scotty's customs after a pint or two and when we were safely back in camp, was to stand stock still, shade his eyes with his hand, scan the horizon — be it rows of huts or barrack blocks — and declaim "I see no ships!" Why he did this, we had absolutely no idea and, possibly, neither had he, but we always roared with laughter.

If there was a camp dance in progress when we got back, we would join in, often as a linked-up foursome, just swaying in time to the beat of the band; a little tipsy island in the midst of the gyrating couples. Not exactly conduct appropriate to the dizzy rank of corporal, you might think? And perhaps you would be right. But the war was over, we'd won it and while there was still a necessary amount of discipline, we were all marking time, as it were, while we waited for our release dates. I had company, too, as Scotty was also a corporal.

However, neither he nor Harry was in evidence on New Year's Eve, 1945 — they must have been on leave — and we were in the company of Don and Geoff — the "retired" aircrew. We had no clear idea of what we were going to do, other than to see the New Year in with a dram; Heather, you will remember, was a Scot.

Naturally, we went to a pub, in Warrington this time. We'd hardly been there five minutes before a charming, middle-aged couple came over and chatted to us, then insisted upon taking us all back to their house to see in the New Year in style. Once there, and to my great surprise, although probably not Heather's, we discovered that they had already prepared a wonderful buffet supper for us. Apparently, they had gone out with the express purpose of finding some service personnel and taking them back, and we had been the lucky ones. Their generous action was typical of the North Country hospitality we met everywhere.

Besides our regular pub, there was also a civilian club up the road to which Heather and I were invited one evening. I can't remember who issued the invitation, but I do remember that there seemed to be an unlimited amount of alcohol, mostly spirits. Somewhat unwisely, we chose to drink gin; a drink that I, at least, was utterly unacquainted with. You can guess the rest.

When we eventually tottered back to camp, it was very late and we found our hut in total darkness. Letting ourselves in at the back door — an unwise choice since we slept at the far end — we were faced with two rows of iron bedsteads stretching away into the distance with only a strip of polished linoleum between. Could we make it to our bed spaces without falling flat in our faces and thus waking the entire hut, including the sergeant in charge who also slept at the far end? Other than spending the night in the ablutions — and we weren't quite far gone enough for that — we had no option but to try. We removed our shoes — again an unwise choice since our stockinged feet now had no purchase on the slippery floor. However, nothing daunted, we set off and managed to ricochet from one bed-end to another like two yachts tacking in a cross-channel breeze. It was really quite exhilarating until Heather dropped one of her shoes. Instantly, we froze, but apart from a few drowsy mutterings,

140

everyone slept on including the sergeant in her own little cubicle.

My stomach didn't really recover for a good month, but at least there was one important bonus — I'd finished with gin!

There was one other never-to-be-forgotten day while I was at Padgate and a much happier one. Scotty and I, finding ourselves with the same day off, decided to spend it in New Brighton; a sort of mini-Blackpool at the mouth of the Mersey where it flows into the Irish Sea.

Neither of us had been on a proper seaside holiday for at least four years; few people had. When service personnel had leave, they usually went home and anyway, most of the beaches had stakes driven into them to foil any possible invasion. So it was like compressing four years of summer holidays into one glorious June day.

Licking enormous ice-cream cones, we strolled along the promenade, rode donkeys on the sands — I fell off mine, a narrow WAAF skirt not being the most practical of riding attire — ate enormous plates of fish and chips and had our photographs taken by an enterprising lad who snapped holiday makers as they strolled in the sunshine, then sold them the result. I still have ours — now a much-faded, sepia print showing the blurred outlines of a tall, RAF corporal and a diminutive WAAF corporal, both grinning broadly.

Wandering at random, relaxed and happy, we found ourselves alongside the funfair. Would I, Scotty enquired wistfully, like to have a go on the Big Dipper?

I followed his gaze and felt my stomach curdle. I had always hated heights and speed, and the little cars rattling along the track high above our heads, seemed to be the epitome of both.

"You'd be all right," Scotty assured me. "You can always hang on to me. And anyway, you'd be strapped in." We were having such a lovely day that it seemed a pity to spoil it by jibbing at the last fence, so to speak. So I gave in.

Of course we were strapped in, and of course a heavy bar was slotted into place in front of us once we'd taken our seats in our own little car. And at first, it was really pleasant; a gradual climb until we were high over New Brighton with the sunlit Wirral stretching out ahead. But then our speed suddenly increased, we whizzed around a couple of bends and the Wirral disappeared to be replaced by the sea which now seemed, to my jaundiced eye, to be glittering in the most malevolent fashion. And then came what was probably considered to be the highlight of the ride but for me was a moment of sheer terror which I have never forgotten. The track ahead seemed to disappear into thin air and our speed, if anything, increased. Clearly, we were about to hurtle into eternity. I turned my face into the comforting warmth of Scotty's tunic, and his arm came around me.

At this point, I feel it would be nice and in true romantic tradition, if I could report a blinding flash of light as I gazed into his eyes and forgot all about our impending doom as I realised that he was the love of my life. He, of course, would feel exactly the same. And our lips would meet . . .

As it was, all I felt was one of his tunic buttons pressing painfully into my nose and my stomach threatening to dispose of my recently eaten fish and chips. When our car finally shuddered to a halt, and I'd peeled myself off him, he said,

"All right now, old girl?" And I, in return, gave him a sheepish grin and said, if he didn't mind, I'd like to sit down for a bit — preferably on something that didn't move. So much for romance!

CHAPTER
SEVENTEEN

It was while I was at Padgate, the war safely over and discipline relaxed among those awaiting demob that many of us began to lead a life of crime.

Because we knew roughly when our demob would be, it became ever more irksome to be killing time, doing very little, and certainly not the jobs that most people had joined up for, when loved ones at home, particularly wives, were longing for our return. Thirty-six and forty-eight hour passes were like gold dust and far too infrequent to satisfy most people.

However, with pads of blank passes easily available in the Orderly Room, it was easy enough for personnel to extract the odd few and smuggle them out to distribute among their friends. The only snag was that, in order to make them valid, they required an official signature. It was then that the forger's expertise reared its ugly — or, some might say, gifted — head. Many people discovered a hitherto unsuspected talent for this nefarious practice and became instantly popular.

Looking back, the risk of discovery was slight. The only time when you might have had to produce the pass was if you were apprehended by the Military Police while you were, so to speak, in transit, and if you kept your head down on railway stations and did your best to avoid them — they were easy to spot as they always hunted in pairs and, as well as an unsmiling expression, wore red bands around their caps — there was no reason why they should take any notice of you.

However, legitimizing one's absence from camp was one thing; finding the money for the train fare was another, since the passes didn't include a travel warrant.

After four years of war, the railways must have been in a bad way with rolling stock in sore need of replacement. But this never occurred to us. The railway companies were a faceless institution that was considered fair game to beat. I don't think it occurred to people that they were being dishonest — it was just another aspect of "them" and "us", rather in the same way that the WAAF had nicked coal from the RAF stockpile at Benson.

The system most people used was simple and probably foolproof. Certainly, I never heard of it failing. It involved an initial lay-out of the cost of a return ticket home, a return ticket to the next station down the line from your departure point and a similar one from your home station. Thus equipped, you were, so to speak, legitimate throughout, having your main ticket to show to an inspector should one appear while you were en route — a rare occurrence in those days — and only giving up your secondary ticket at the barrier when leaving at either end and these weren't always manned.

All it cost, after the initial outlay, was the purchase of replacement secondary tickets, a negligible amount compared with the total fare. Perhaps people saw it as a legitimate payback for the many journeys they had made during the war when they'd often had to stand up in draughty corridors or squat uncomfortably on their cases.

However, whatever the vicissitudes, I loved those wartime journeys home, especially when I was stationed at Benson. The main Great Western Railway line from Paddington to South Wales was through Reading where there was a very good Forces canteen on the station. My connection from Wallingford always got me there in time to call in for a mug of coffee and a hot dog (not that we called them that before the Americans arrived!) which set me up for the journey. Then, if I was lucky, I would find a corner seat and wait for the familiar landmarks to appear. The lush embankments in the Thames Valley were always a source of great delight especially in spring when they were thick with primroses. Next came my old friends the Wittenham Clumps, seen now from a completely different angle but clearly visible on the horizon. There was little then of much significance to me, and I would read my book or chat to other travellers. Chatting to other travellers was always fascinating during the war. United by a common cause and all of us, on the whole, enduring the same hardships, our normal "British" inhibitions vanished completely with the most welcome results. Civilians were always interested in life in the Services and where one or two members of the Services were gathered together, it was always entertaining to exchange our different experiences of service life. Sadly, this admirable situation didn't last long after hostilities were over.

When the train neared the Welsh border, all open windows would have to be laboriously pulled up on their leather straps while we rattled through the Severn Tunnel. If this wasn't done, you would be liberally spattered with smuts blowing back from the engine. Once through the tunnel, the windows would go down again, and we were in Wales. From then on, it was a matter of reliving my childhood memories of my father taking my brother and me to see our grandmother in Swansea. As we came into Newport, there would be the familiar row of terrace houses displaying Beecham Pills advertisements. Once again, I speculated on how much each house owner was being paid for the advertisement. However, since it was rare in those days for people to own their own houses, it would probably have been the landlord who would have profited. It would also have been interesting to know just how many rail travellers decided to try Beecham Pills as a result!

When leaving Newport, we'd always had to gaze seaward in order to catch a glimpse of the suspension bridge, and then we had the steelworks of Port Talbot to look forward to. If we were lucky, there would be a furnace with its doors wide open on white-hot heat or a glowing ingot of molten ore. This could be particularly spectacular at night in wartime when the rest of the town would be in darkness. Soon after, there would be glimpses of sand dunes and the enticing smells of sand and sea.

Finally, on wartime journeys, we would chug into Wind Street station and there would be my mother, waiting at the barrier. If it was very late and the buses had stopped, there would be a three mile walk home but otherwise, we would board a Number 22 bus for Cockett and get off at Cockett Church. (We lived next door to the church and were frequently mistaken for the Vicarage.) Then it was home with a lovely warm bed at night and, best of all perhaps, staying in it as long as I wanted to next day. I probably even had breakfast in it, courtesy of my dear mother.

Travelling home from Padgate had quite a different feel to it, perhaps because I had to change trains a couple of times and could therefore never settle. However, I did develop a most unlikely affection for Crewe station which, in my experience was possibly one of the dirtiest stations in Great Britain but was staffed by some of the kindest people. When going home, I had little time to linger there between trains but going back to camp was a different matter. In order to give myself as much time as possible at home, I always travelled late in the day and would reach Crewe long after the last connection to Warrington had left. But after a reviving cup of tea and a bun, I would make my way to the platform where there was a "Ladies Only" waiting room and the most welcoming coal fire I had ever seen in my life. Sometimes there would be a couple of other females there, but it was never crowded, and I could always stretch out on one of the shiny, horse-hair couches that lined the walls, draw my greatcoat collar up around my ears and sleep the sleep of the young and healthy. Sometime in the night, a porter would knock respectfully on the door before coming in to make up the fire and would always appear again to alert me to the departure of the so-called "milk train" to Warrington, which would get me back to camp in plenty of time for 0800 hours when my pass expired.

Another journey I enjoyed while at Padgate was by cross-country bus to Chester. My mother had grown up in a village a few miles from Chester and had often told me about its ancient walls and mediaeval houses and, particularly, its beautiful sandstone cathedral.

As with my trips to Oxford, I would stay at the excellent YWCA and wander around as the spirit took me. I walked around the walls, gazing out over the water meadows along the River Dee towards Eaton Hall, the seat of the Dukes of Westminster, where my father had convalesced during the First World War. I ambled through the covered mediaeval walkways, now housing rather expensive shops and went to morning service in the Cathedral where I was entranced by the combination of choir, soaring architecture and the brilliant colours of the vestments. It was easy to believe in God under such conditions. Another wonderful spectacle I enjoyed in Chester was seeing Laurence Olivier in *Henry V*.

Besides these visual goodies, there was also a brand new NAAFI Club which offered excellent food in almost palatial surroundings. It almost made me query my decision not to sign on as a regular in the

WAAF, an option which was open to all of us, but which few of us took up. Members of the regular peacetime Air Force seemed to take it all so seriously!

CHAPTER
EIGHTEEN

It was with very mixed feelings that I eventually organized my own demob party. Heather, having earned herself an earlier release date by virtue of being married, had already gone. Those of us who were left rallied round, and it was a happy but sad occasion. Scotty "saw no ships" for the last time from the cookhouse steps, and Gordon presented me with a brilliant sketch of the Section peopled by all my friends, all of whom had written kind messages on the back. It is still one of my most treasured possessions.

Next day, I set off for Wythall to be officially demobbed and was presented with my demob book which contained, among other documents, a statement that I had been an efficient and reliable teleprinter op. I was also given a cheque for twelve pounds with which to buy civilian clothes. The men were actually given a demob suit which, I understand, was put to various uses, among them being a snazzy suit for a scarecrow! But this, I think, was an exception. Many of them were worn to work and lasted for quite a while. With my allowance I proposed to buy myself a bicycle, George having been honourably retired when I left Benson.

Travelling home in uniform for the very last time, I was aware of an enormous sense of anti-climax. Admittedly, I had two whole months of demob leave ahead of me which would be spent cycling up the Wye Valley with Jess, one of my old Post Office friends, spending time in Abergavenny with old school friends and a holiday in North Devon with David. But I also knew that life would never be quite the same again.

The war was a terrible thing, but since it had to happen there was nowhere else I would rather have been than in the WAAF. And, in many ways, the war brought out the best in people. We were all much kinder to each other, and home comforts were really appreciated, not taken for granted. And we didn't moan — well, not much! — we just got on with the job.

It had been fun to meet people from different walks of life; I remember an afternoon spent picking up potatoes from the middle of Benson airfield in the company of a charming young man who was determined to make a career in the theatre once the war was over. I think he probably made it for he had all sorts of useful contacts, and I wish I could remember his name!

In peacetime, I would never have known the Macs at Cherry Trees as well as I did. Class structure in England before the war was much more rigidly defined than it is now, and our respective circles would never have intertwined in any social sense.

Because you were in uniform, most civilians would bend over backwards to be nice to you. Shopkeepers would find little luxuries like bars of perfumed soap "under the counter" and pass them over when no-one else was in the shop. And business men, on long train journeys, would insist upon paying for your mid-morning coffee in the restaurant car while they told you about their sons and daughters.

I was no longer going to have access to Naafi shops where lipsticks and face cream could often be found at reasonable prices. And free cigarettes would no longer be issued.

Although I would never have put it into so many words, I had never really expected to have to go back to the Post Office. In my dreams, Cupid, in the shape of some dazzling young man in uniform, would have carried me off to some wonderfully romantic life, but here I was, coming back to pick up the strands of my old life practically where I had left them. Admittedly, I had great hopes that David and I would eventually end up together, but our future was still shrouded in uncertainty.

I remember that one of my old Post Office friends who had joined the Wrens after I had left for the WAAF, had actually come home with, so to speak, two proposals of marriage under her belt. I think she had been posted to somewhere like Scapa Flo where the ratio of men to women was something like a hundred to one — or was it a thousand to one? Not only was there a young naval rating wanting to marry her but also a rather dashing young naval officer. In the end, the latter won the day, and I was invited to their wedding — a very enjoyable affair, which was the beginning of a very successful married life.

However, there could be no doubt of my mother's pleasure at welcoming me back home into the nest. We both missed Bill and mourned his loss all over again, but she once told me that she was so grateful that she still had me,

"Otherwise," she said, "I would probably have lost contact with young people altogether." From then on, she was included in as many of my outings as possible.

Perhaps the biggest change that civilian life would offer was the absence of contact with people of my own age from the moment of waking up in the morning to going to bed at night. Now, at my advanced age, there is nothing I like more than waking up in the morning to solitude and only the company of my dog unless I choose to make it otherwise but then, in my early twenties, it was great to have good friends immediately available; to decide, if one wasn't due on watch, what to do with the morning and, sometimes, the rest of the day.

But my good friend, Joan Isaac, was still in Swansea. There was much to look forward to. But there was one thing I was quite sure about; I wouldn't have missed the last four years for anything.

CHAPTER
NINETEEN

My demob leave was an unqualified success. Looking back, I am amazed at how much I crammed into it. My mother didn't want to go anywhere but was simply content to have me back at home — not that I was there very much.

I began by going back to Abergavenny to stay with my old friend, Christine Jones. Once more, I climbed the Deri, picnicked by the River Usk and met up with Bill's old school friend, Guffin, alias Stan Jones, now demobbed from the army and studying to complete his accountancy exams. He took me for lunch at a pub that he and Bill had frequented and then for a memorable drive up into the Black Mountains where we lay on smooth sheep-nibbled turf and talked about Bill. Afterwards, he drove us to Gilwern to meet up with Peg Powell, another old friend of mine, who was about to marry Guthrie Cooper, a flight lieutenant in the Air Force. All in all, it was a good day.

While in Abergavenny, I also spent my clothing allowance on a brand new Raleigh bicycle of which I was extremely proud and which I would take back to Swansea in the guard's van. Christine had recently become engaged to a young farmer called Stephen

Watkins and before I left, I had arranged to come back for Monmouthshire's first post-war Hunt Ball — with David, if he could manage it. This raised the problem of what I was to wear as a long, evening dress would be obligatory, and I had never owned such a garment. While I had, of course, been issued with clothing coupons, they were extremely precious, and I had no wish to fritter them away upon a garment that I was unlikely to wear again for a while. So the "items for sale" column in the local newspaper were hastily scanned. And there it was — "one bridesmaid's dress in gold taffeta, worn once, price twelve shillings and sixpence" and the right size. The only problem was — the owner lived in Hereford, a good twenty miles away. But there was a good bus service and it was too good an opportunity to miss. I knew Hereford fairly well, found the right house with little effort and scooped up my bargain. It was a bargain, even though the puff sleeves and decorous, heart-shaped neckline were not the last word in "haute couture" — but at least it was long!

The purchase completed, I found I had time to kill before the next bus back to Abergavenny and went into a café for a cup of coffee. Imagine my astonishment when I heard a familiar voice, easily distinguishable above the buzz of conversation. It belonged to Molly Murray, Bill's old girl friend, in animated conversation with a couple of elderly ladies who — there was no doubt of it! — were very deaf indeed.

She had her back to me and, anyway, I had no wish to break up the conversation, so I waited outside until she came out, minus the two elderly ladies. Her astonishment was equal to mine. When the war ended, she had met up again with an army medical officer whose driver she had been and who had spent most of the war in a German POW camp. They had married and were now living in Hereford where he was in general practice. She insisted upon taking me home to meet him and then, as I still had to catch a bus, we exchanged addresses and promised to keep in touch.

Before The Hunt Ball, which was good fun, I had cycled up the Wye Valley with an old Post Office friend, Jessie Hunt. We stayed at Youth Hostels and eventually reached Stratford-upon-Avon — clearly, we had abandoned the Wye at some point — where we went to the theatre to see, if I remember correctly, *Twelfth Night*. The return journey was through the Welsh Border country to Abergavenny and into the Black Mountains where it rained solidly. One of my abiding memories of the trip was the tin of Cheddar cheese that an aunt in New Zealand had included in a food parcel she had sent at the end of the war to help eke out our rations. The taste of that rich Cheddar on a tongue that hadn't experienced anything like it for five years was exquisite. When we eventually reached Swansea, it was to find David waiting for me, on a short leave from a nearby airfield.

A few days at Cherry Trees with the Macs was, of course, a "must". Her son, Gordon, was home on leave from the 8th Army; a sun-tanned, fair-haired Apollo who, in spite of numerous girl friends vying for his company, found time to take me out for a very grown-up lunch in a very smart hotel. There was also a young medical student — a distant cousin of Mr Mac's — called Sandy who was just passing through on his motorbike on his way home to Carmarthenshire. His route lay through Swansea, and I ended up going with him, riding pillion and enveloped in an enormous bell tent of a waterproof — it rained all the way! Once I'd realised I had to lean over into the bend on corners and not outwards, I found it quite exhilarating although it needed the united efforts of both Sandy and my mother to get me back into a standing position once we'd reached home!

The final part of my leave was spent with David; at his family home for the first few days and then at a country pub in North Devon where we stayed for a week. David's parents were very nice to me, as was his younger sister, but I was conscious that they would have preferred David to wait a while before "settling down" which was something that I certainly didn't want to do.

But Devon was perfect. For the first time since we'd met, we were completely free agents. With the help of a benevolent landlady with a tendency to mother us and who provided us with enormous packed lunches, we explored the Devon countryside, watching buzzards circling above the River Torridge, into whose icy depths we had just plunged and drinking cider in ancient quay-side pubs in Bideford and Appledore. Once we caught a train to Bude where David, greatly daring, swam in the sea but decided later that he had probably chosen the place where Bude's effluent was discharged!

I may be maligning the local authority of the time, but there were certainly an awful lot of squawking seagulls weaving about around David's head!

All in all, it was a very satisfactory, peacetime holiday and we were both sad to see the end of it. But it was fun to catch the paddle steamer from Minehead to Swansea and be escorted in mid-channel by a school of porpoises. There followed several days of being thoroughly spoilt by my mother.

Although the war in the Far East had now ended, David still had several months of service life before he was demobbed and I, of course, had the Post Office to go back to. Not that I was exactly looking forward to it. But before that, I managed to fit in a few days in London, staying with Heather and Dennis in their tiny flat in Harrow. They were both out at work during the day, so I was able to look up some old friends.

Margaret and William were now living in South Norwood, so I travelled out to Croydon and was met at the station by William who was working there for the Inland Revenue and had managed an extended lunch hour in order to meet me on his bike.

He put me on the bus that would stop at the end of their road, told the conductor where I should be put off, paid my fare and then hopped back on his bike and followed the bus. I'd been a little worried as to how I should get on with William on an informal basis. Would I — heaven forbid! — call him "sir" from force of habit and barely restrain my right hand from rising to the salute? Would I instinctively stand to attention when spoken to? But I needn't have worried. William in grey

159

flannels and a Harris tweed sports jacket, fair hair blowing in the breeze as he peddled after the bus, occasionally lifting a hand to give me a reassuring wave, was quite a different person from Squadron Leader Ellis, O/C Signals Section, Benson.

Margaret, heavily pregnant with Heather, her firstborn to whom I was to be godmother, was radiant. Once William had finished his lunch, thanked me for coming and got back on his bike, Margaret and I settled down for a good gossip. Married life was suiting her and what, in retrospect, had been a leap in the dark was clearly turning out to be a great success.

On another day, I met up with May O'Shea. She was working at Grosvenor House in Park Lane as a staff supervisor and had instructed me to report to the Reception Desk, and she would immediately come down and take me up to her room for tea. Nothing could have been more simple, but I was still a little overawed by the opulence of the place and was grateful that at least she wasn't working at the larger and, to me, even more intimidating, Dorchester, next door.

But May hadn't changed at all, in spite of looking incredibly efficient in her smart uniform. Once again, we had a great chat, and I was able to give her an update on the Ellises. It was May who, on Margaret's wedding morning, had known exactly how to arrange her wedding veil so that she looked beautiful instead of "frumpy" as her mother-in-law-to-be had thought she should. She was as pleased as me that everything had turned out so well.

160

I went back to Swansea and Post Office routine, thinking how glamorous it must be to work in London and, best of all, in the West End. Swansea, slowly recovering from the ravages of the blitz seemed dull and dreary by comparison.

CHAPTER
TWENTY

Apparently, in my absence, I had become eligible for counter duties. I had very mixed feelings about it. Dealing with the public was interesting in itself but mathematics, even basic adding-up, had never been one of my strengths. However, I was dispatched to the Counter Training School at Shrewsbury for a fortnight and managed to pass out at a sufficiently high level. While there, I spent a weekend in Hereford with Molly, which was great fun. They were now living outside Hereford in Tony's family home and waiting for the arrival of their firstborn.

Although I'd passed out of the course, I found that facing the public was quite another matter. I shall never forget my first customer. She'd made a very simple request for "six twopenny ha'penny stamps, please". (Two and a half pence, in old money, was then the price of a 1st class stamp.)

A simple request, you might think. But in my state of extreme nerves, I was quite incapable of any mental arithmetic. Surreptitiously, I did a quick sum on a scrap of paper under the counter.

"One and three, please," I requested as I tore off the stamps from the huge sheets I had in my stamp book.

After that, I felt much better and dealt with complicated tasks like issuing money orders with gay insouciance. Probably too much gay insouciance since I never once, throughout the eighteen months I spent on counter duties, managed to "balance my drawer" — something that counter staff had to do every week. Regularly, I had to "make up" my drawer to the right amount from my own money. Sometimes to the tune of £5 — a great deal of money in those days.

However, salvation was within my grasp, and I eventually managed to scrape through the Civil Service exam to become a clerical officer. Where, I was asked, would I like to be posted? There was never any choice since David was now back at Oxford, studying to complete his degree. So I was assigned to the Potato and Carrot Division of the Ministry of Agriculture, Fisheries and Food at New Marston in the suburb of Oxford. With my wartime experience of YWCA hostels behind me, I opted to stay at the YWCA in the Banbury Road. Having, by then, reached the massive age of twenty-six, I was a few years older than most of the other residents, but that didn't seem to matter, and I quickly made some very good friends, both there and at the office. This was as well since soon after arriving in Oxford, David and I split up.

It was sad, of course. I had asked if I could be sent to Oxford precisely because I wanted to be near David in order to marry him and live there with him until he got his degree. But it didn't take many days to discover that the magic of our relationship had gone.

We had been out for the evening — I think to the Playhouse where Oxford's excellent repertory company would have been performing. He had walked me back to the hostel afterwards, and we were standing under the branches of a huge almond tree, the light from a nearby street lamp turning its mass of blossom into an iridescent pink canopy above our heads. Did he, I enquired bluntly, really want to marry me? In hindsight, from the vantage point of so many years later, I am interested to note that while I had made myself face the fact that things had gone sadly awry, I wasn't brave enough to say I didn't want to marry him. Perhaps, deep down, I hoped he would throw his arms around me and assure me of his undying love thus, hopefully, rekindling mine in the process. But it wasn't quite like that. Admittedly, he protested that of course he wanted to marry me, but there was no passion there. He could have been protesting that of course he wanted Aunt Mabel to come for Christmas or didn't mind little Freddie playing with his precious train set! However, by then it was nearly time for the YWCA's strict curfew to come into operation, so we agreed hastily to meet on the following evening, and I went in. But not, needless to say, to sleep for some time.

By the following evening, the scenario had changed completely. Taking, as it were, the masculine initiative, David now became the lead player in our little drama. Patiently, as if talking to a young, seventeen-year-old, he explained that marriage was a serious business — surprise, surprise! — and not to be undertaken lightly. It was, in all cases, an unpredictable gamble and certainly not one to be considered unless the participants had at least thought they were made for each other. It certainly shouldn't be entered into, he assured me more than a shade pompously, if there was the slightest doubt as to its success. So, to continue with our marriage plans would be foolhardy indeed.

I listened to all this with a mixture of intense annoyance but also of extreme sadness. No doubt the war had given an emotional edge to our relationship but, whatever the reasons it was one that, for a time, had made us both very happy so it was sad to see it go — but inevitable. As I've already tried to explain, David had acquired far more social poise and polish than I, and it was now beginning to show. Sadly, it was my mother, I think, who suffered the most. When I wrote to her, telling her what had happened, her reply could have been written by the one whose romance had been broken off; it certainly wasn't one offering consolation to a sorrowing daughter! Maybe, I had sounded too philosophical and not in the least heartbroken in my letter but clearly, she saw herself as the wounded party. I think that she'd seen David as a sort of adopted son who would, eventually, take the place of the one she had lost.

For several weeks after we'd broken up, life, to put it mildly, was not a bowl of cherries and wasn't helped by my suddenly seeing David in the company of another girl just a few days after we'd parted company. I was walking back to the hostel after work and taking the scenic route beside the river through the University Parks, when I saw a punt moored to the bank under a willow tree with a couple sitting in it. I gave them a cursory glance as I passed and then, to my horror, saw that the young man was David. He glanced up at the same moment and for a few dreadful moments, our eyes locked, before I managed a sort of sickly grin and carried on my way, my heart pounding. He managed nothing at all and that, perhaps, hurt most of all. But I suppose he was too shocked.

However, I was young, Oxford was a beautiful city and living in the YWCA provided plenty of diversions. Nearly all the girls were two or three years younger than I was, but that didn't seem to matter. The "New Look", which consisted of long and very full skirts below a nipped-in waist, as unlike wartime austerity as possible, was just coming in to fashion, and the hostel sewing machine whirred non-stop. We had a sort of communal wardrobe, borrowing each other's clothes and jewellery if anyone had an important date. Saturday night dances, heavily attended by male undergraduates, were held at the Carfax Assembly Rooms and often resulted in tea in someone's rooms next day. It was rare for any permanent relationship to develop as a result, but it was all very pleasant.

I met a young man from Ruskin College who tried to get amorous on his landlady's hearthrug — he was in digs — and as a result burned a sizeable hole in it by knocking over an electric fire. I'm afraid he lost out on all counts, as I didn't feel at all amorous about him, and I can only imagine his landlady's wrath the next day.

The office was fun, too. My job was in the Potato and Carrot Division of the Ministry of Agriculture, Fisheries and Food and was concerned, basically, in keeping tabs on every potato grown in the U.K. Every serious potato grower was sent a census return upon which they were legally obliged to record their acreage and the variety of potato they had planted. It wasn't what you could remotely call fascinating, but its lack of glamour was more than compensated for by the staff who performed it.

Variety was the keyword; the little army of form checkers I was responsible for included a couple of car mechanics, an ex-actress, now permanently "resting", whose son was an Oxford don (she had great stories about Gaiety Girls who had married into the aristocracy at the turn of the century), a recently married young housewife, several elderly widows and a delightful ex-RAF man called Sydney, whose wife, Betty, worked in the same building in a much more senior position than his. They commuted each day from the village of Brill in a vintage Bentley of which Sydney was inordinately proud.

Soon after I had arrived, I was invited for the weekend to their lovely old cottage which they shared with their three-legged cat. Brill, I found to be a lovely village built around several acres of common land on which, of course, no-one could build. On the highest point of the common was — and still is — a well-preserved windmill.

It was an interesting time to be in Oxford; undergraduates whose university careers had been interrupted by the war, were now coming back — like David — so that the student populace was an interesting mix of those coming straight from school in the usual way and seasoned war veterans coming back from the Services. I was fortunate in that there was a middle-aged Oxford graduate working at the office who could obtain passes to the Visitors' Gallery at the Union Debating Society and who often gave them to me, so that I became a regular observer of the debates.

The officers were an interesting collection and, if I remember correctly, consisted of Peter Kirk as president — son of the current bishop of Oxford — Ken Tynan as secretary — later to become a well-known theatre critic — and Tony Benn as treasurer — then the Right Honourable Anthony Wedgwood Benn. Apart from some very interesting debates, I particularly remember the sartorial peccadilloes of Ken Tynan. He once made a grand entry, to rousing cheers, clad in a lilac-coloured suit and being pushed in a wheelbarrow.

And then, in May, I made a friendship which still endures and which was to have a profound influence on my Oxford life. I was catching a Green Line coach up to London one Saturday just after midday when I'd finished work (we worked Saturday mornings as a matter of course in those days). I was to spend the weekend with my old school friend Elisabeth, who had married a Polish Airforce officer and was now living with him in Hampstead. The coach was scheduled to leave from the Cape of Good Hope pub on the Cowley Road where it joins the Plain. I was standing outside on the pavement when the pub door opened and out came a smart young woman whom I estimated — correctly, I later discovered — to be a few years older than me. She didn't look in the least like the sort of person one would expect to be having a midday tipple in a city pub — remember that this was 1948 and "respectable" woman didn't generally do that sort of thing. Nowadays, thank heaven, no-one would think twice about it.

However, she gave me a beaming smile and asked if I too, was waiting for the London coach? We were soon deep in conversation, and I discovered that she'd gone into the pub to check on the time of the coach and found it highly amusing that I thought she'd been "knocking it back".

Naturally, we sat next to each other on the coach, and she told me that her name was Margaret Martin and that she worked at the Churchill Hospital in Oxford as a medical secretary. She also lived just around the corner from the hostel, in Park Town, a lovely double crescent of elegant Georgian houses where she had a flat, and she was going home to Sidcup for the weekend. She was also, during the weekend, intending to end an affair with an army major whose feelings she desperately didn't want to hurt. Naturally, one thing led to another, and I soon found myself telling her all about David. By the time the coach had reached Victoria Coach Station, we were firm friends and had agreed to look out for each other on Paddington station when we returned to Oxford by train on Sunday evening; presumably, there wasn't a suitable coach.

I've always remembered that weekend because Elisabeth and Jerzy had got tickets for a concert at the Albert Hall. I don't remember either the orchestra or the conductor, but I do remember that Tchaikowsky's 1812 was in their repertoire. At the end of it, one timpanist gave such an energetic performance that one of his drumsticks flew out of his hand, performed a near parabola across the stage and nearly knocked over the conductor. The resulting gasp from the audience nearly drowned the final, crashing chords.

I also remember a gorgeous taffeta evening dress of exotic peacock blues and greens that Elisabeth passed on to me because she'd grown out of it. It had narrow, bootlace straps and, to me, was the height of glamour. I remember that I wore it, to great effect, at the office Christmas Dance.

Margaret and I didn't meet up at Paddington but found each other at Oxford station and walked home together. From then on, life took on a whole new perspective. She had lived in Oxford for some time and knew lots of people. My diary for that year shows a crowded social life — punting on the river with Barbara and Joyce, two of my hostel friends, tennis with Margaret, frequent visits to the theatre and cinema, cycle rides out into the Oxfordshire countryside and, most exciting of all, a holiday in Italy with Margaret.

CHAPTER
TWENTY-ONE

Going abroad for the first time, unless experienced at a very early age, is always an unforgettable experience. But when it happens after years of war-time deprivation, it is a revelation. Margaret and I decided upon Lake Garda in Northern Italy as our destination. Although no longer a student, Margaret still belonged to the National Union of Students and, as such, qualified to go on their holidays.

The meeting point was the Boat Train departure platform on Victoria Station. We were a motley collection. There was a charming solicitor called Edgar, not long out of the army, an attractive female undergraduate from Lady Margaret Hall, Oxford called Veronica, several other young students, male and female and three male medical students from Queen's College, Cambridge. I can't recall any specific leader, so we must have been considered bright enough to get ourselves to Newhaven and the cross-channel steamer to Dieppe and then survive the long train journey across France, via Paris and Dijon, and to arrive eventually at Torbole on Lake Garda.

Right from the start, Margaret and I and the three medical students, gravitated towards each other. Two of them, Ian and Eric, came from the north of England and Andy from Southampton. Margaret was the only seasoned, pre-war traveller among us.

It would be many years before air travel became the norm and, as far as I'm concerned, travelling by rail and sea has always been the most enjoyable. I find it so much more satisfying to experience Continental travel by degrees. To have breakfast in Rome, say, and lunch back home in England is far too much of a culture shock to me. So, I shall never forget my first whiff of France as I walked off the ferry, grateful that the travel-sickness pills Margaret had advised me to take had made my first Channel crossing a pleasant affair; it was an unforgettable mix of Gaulois cigarettes and garlic, strong coffee and even stronger cheese. It was heady stuff! And then there were the trains; great, panting monsters waiting for our arrival at the quayside. Clambering up into the carriages was, for me with my short legs, like climbing Everest. We managed to find our reserved compartments and settled down for our overnight journey to Milan where we would have to change for the last leg of the journey.

I think there was a restaurant car of sorts, but a meal in it would have cost a small fortune and anyway, under Margaret's expert guidance, I had come well-equipped with sandwiches and drinks which we were happy to share. The stations we stopped at — my diary mentions Aix-les-Bains, Modane and Turin before we reached Milan — had several food vendors, happy to serve us with whatever they had on offer, but "foreign food" was still somewhat suspect in our insular eyes. Cut off from

Europe by four years of war, we still viewed Continental hygiene with the deepest suspicion. We felt far safer with our cheese sandwiches and thermoses!

Nobody slept much that night as we chugged steadily on — safety not speed was the maxim for French rolling stock at that time, like the British, it must still have been recovering from the effects of wartime over-use. Passports had to be produced when we crossed into Italy, but we didn't mind that at all as it meant another stamp upon their pristine pages. Looking at that old passport now, I see that I acquired at least four stamps during that holiday which must have pleased me enormously at the time.

Cross-country Italian trains, we discovered next day, weren't nearly as comfortable as the French. However, the discomfort of their slatted, wooden seats complete with wooden backs, was more than compensated for by the interesting variety of our fellow travellers. As we jogged through Lombardy from one small town to the next, we acquired a couple of priests, sweating profusely in their dark, heavy suits, several soldiers from the Italian army going home on leave and celebrating with copious swigs from bottles of Chianti and countless country women going to market with baskets laden with vegetables, butter and extremely smelly cheeses. It was enough to keep our drooping eyelids at half-mast for most of the journey.

But we were a very tired little group that eventually arrived in the early evening at the village of Desenzano on the shores of Lake Garda, to be met by a guy called Chris who was to be our guide and mentor for the next ten days. In our comparatively youthful eyes, he was a very old gentleman but, in hindsight, he was probably in his early sixties. Snapshots show a tall, balding man who, with great panache, wore a monocle rammed into his eye even when wearing shorts, as he was for most of the time.

He had been marooned in Italy at the beginning of the war and now, he couldn't contemplate living anywhere else. So he had taken up permanent residence in the hotel where we were stay in Torbole, further down the lake. We were taken there by the coach that he had arranged for us, and while we were waiting to be allocated our rooms, Andy and I crossed the road, took off our shoes and paddled our hot, tired feet in the lake. It was magic! Then it was up to our rooms and oblivion under the downy billows of my first duvet experience.

Margaret and I were sharing a room and, the next morning, woke to a room full of sunlight and the gentle murmur of lapping water at the lake shore, which reminded me of a Yeats poem. I threw back my duvet and tottered, bleary-eyed, to the window. The view was like something out of a child's fairy story, and I doubt I can do it justice.

Except for the narrow band of the coastal road, there was nothing between the lake and us. Its colours were like the wings of myriad blue butterflies; pale, cerulean blue merged with streaks of sapphire, turquoise and deep, deep indigo, and all sparkling like diamonds under the rays of the early morning sun. Far away across the water, were the hazy contours of the

174

mountains rising from the opposite shore. Further down the lake, I could see the terra cotta tiles of Riva and the dark green foliage of orange and lemon trees.

Margaret soon joined me, and we leaned out of our window, drinking it all in. For years, I had dreamed of "abroad", and now I knew it had been worth waiting for.

Our breakfast, like most of our meals, was eaten outside under a canopy of vine leaves while Chris filled us in with details of the local attractions. About a hundred yards up the road was the Paradiso night club that, provided we patronized it, would stay open until the small hours. Just up the road from the hotel was a small, safe bathing area and a wooden landing stage where rowing boats were available and a paddle steamer called twice daily on its way around the lake, calling at every village.

Riva was a mile or two down the road and on the bus route, if we didn't feel like walking. There, we would find shops, cafés and tennis courts and a proper bathing "plage". And if we wanted to drive up into the hills to explore some of the tiny villages scattered across the hillside, he would be happy to arrange it. The sole purpose of our holiday, he reminded us, was to enjoy ourselves and nothing would be too much trouble to arrange. We were the first party of tourists he was to look after, and he welcomed us with open arms.

As the holiday progressed, it became more and more obvious that the "open arms" were opened just that little bit wider for Margaret than for the rest of us. Although years younger than he, she was still nearest to

175

him in age and had led a more sophisticated life than most of us, although Edgar and I had both been in the Forces. Although Chris didn't normally rise as early as the rest of us and didn't always accompany us on our various daytime activities, he always made a point of sitting next to Margaret at meals and at the Paradiso which we were to frequent on many evenings after dinner.

My diary records long, sun-drenched days and action-packed nights. The day after we arrived, we all walked up the mountainside through olive trees, their leaves shimmering in the heat, their branches laden with ripening fruit, to the tiny, hillside village of Nago where a little shop was selling enormous straw hats. Margaret and I resisted buying them, but Andy and Eric succumbed. Eric, who was very dark, acquired a distinctly Mexican look. I have a snapshot of us all slaking our thirsts at the village fountain.

After dinner, we wandered up the road to the Paradiso and had our first taste of Prosecco, one of the local wines. To my amazement, I found I could dance superbly with Edgar, and not just because of the Presecco but because he seemed to be just the right height and was very light on his feet. Sadly, and wine not withstanding, I could only stumble around the floor with Andy. But it was with him that I found myself paddling in the lake at 2a.m!

Next day — incredibly, after our late night — we were back in the lake for a pre-breakfast dip and — oh, boy, was it cold! My breath was completely taken away as I performed my routine three strokes before having to stand up. But I had such a lovely, tingling sensation all over my body when we came out and ran back to the hotel for hot coffee, it was worth it!

Later, we walked into Riva and watched a basketball match, then bought oranges that had been picked straight from the tree and were incredibly cheap. We also fitted in a visit to the local church and were quite overwhelmed by the number of golden cherubs festooning every corner, peering coyly around pillars and climbing precariously along the window frames. After this cultural exercise, we collapsed into the pavement chairs of a café, and I had my first taste of dark, sweet Vermouth — the first of many. Needless to say, it was back to the Paradiso after dinner.

On the following day, Chris organized a "fleet" of rowing boats for us to visit the opposite shore of the lake. Our boat held Margaret and Chris, Eric, Ian and me; Andy, for some reason, didn't come. Ian and Eric both declared themselves to be experienced oarsmen and took it in turns to row us across. But halfway over and experienced oarsman, notwithstanding, Ian still managed to catch the most enormous crab and whacked me over the head in the process! However, the main thing was that we didn't capsize although the boat rocked alarmingly and, although Ian was allowed to complete the crossing without further mishap, it was Eric who rowed us back! That night, the Paradiso had to manage without us as we all went to bed early in preparation for an early start next day on a special coach trip to Verona.

Sadly, it wasn't an early start for Margaret, as she woke up with a tummy upset and decided she'd better stay in bed. It was a shame she had to miss what turned out to be an eventful day. In the evening, we were booked into the Coliseum for an open-air performance of *Turandot* but before that we went on a shopping spree. Andy bought a record of Paloma Bianca, one of the numbers that was played regularly at the Paradiso, Chris bought a pair of nylon socks and I bought a pair of nylons. In Margaret's absence, Chris invited me to have dinner with him *a deux*, which I enjoyed very much. There was much to be said, I decided, for going out with an older man! We didn't, I'm ashamed to say, visit the house with the balcony where Romeo and Juliet were presumed to have declaimed their famous speeches.

Turandot got off to a flying start but then had to be hastily abandoned when a spectacular thunderstorm suddenly blew up. Actors and audience both had to beat a hasty retreat; the performers to their dressing rooms and the audience to take shelter under the arches surrounding the amphitheatre. I was standing with Andy and Chris, and I remember feeling very hot and thirsty. Andy very kindly went off in search of liquid and came back with a bottle of ice-cold beer which, instead of sipping slowly, I knocked back in seconds. It was the silliest thing I could have done. Immediately, I became aware that I was either going to be very sick indeed or faint. I fainted, falling quite spectacularly into a crumpled heap on the cobbles — so Andy told me later. Fortunately, I came to almost straight away and was hurriedly found a chair on which I sat until the rain stopped, the clouds cleared and a brilliant moon sailed above the auditorium.

The opera restarted, and I remember feeling very wicked and worldly as I sat between Andy and Chris and held hands with both of them! It was a very sleepy collection of people that our coach finally deposited at our hotel at around four o'clock in the morning.

Next day was, of necessity, a quiet one. In the afternoon, Andy and I climbed the hill behind the hotel and sat among the olive trees, talking in a desultory sort of way about our families and our lives back in England. I told him about David, and he told me about his friendship, now finished, with a girl in Cambridge. Now and then, the odd cow, with a bell around her neck, would stroll into view, gaze at us in a speculative sort of way and then continue her grazing. It was very peaceful, and we both fell asleep, our backs against a tree.

That evening, Andy and I strolled beside the lake after dinner and watched summer lightning playing around the mountain tops. Once again, the Paradiso had to function without us as we made up for lost sleep. Margaret, to her great relief and mine, was now completely recovered from her gippy tummy.

Next day, we made yet another early start, rising at six-thirty for a trip around the lake on the daily, scheduled steamer. When we embarked, the lake was shrouded in mist, and it was very cold. For the first time on the holiday, the ubiquitous English cardigans made their appearance, but were soon discarded as the mist cleared and another gloriously sunny day got under way.

We lost track of their number as the steamer stopped at all the little villages around the lake, each with its white campanile soaring from a jumble of terra cotta tiles. Countless crates of chickens and boxes of vegetables were loaded and unloaded. At Sirmione, we disembarked and had lunch after a leisurely bathe in water that was actually warm. I thought of the River Usk at six o'clock in the morning, and it seemed even warmer!

After lunch, we caught the next steamer and resumed our leisurely progress around the lake. Several of us, me included, nodded off after our extremely filling lunch. Sometime on the journey, I must have asked Chris if I could borrow his monocle for I have a snapshot of me obviously holding it in place with extreme difficulty.

That night saw us all back at the Paradiso. Besides "Paloma Bianca", they were very attached to a record they had recently acquired — possibly in our honour — of "That's Why The Lady Is A Tramp". They played it as we all arrived and at frequent intervals throughout the evening. In the end, Chris got so fed up with it, he threatened to throw it in to the lake but was restrained.

Round about midnight, we all started to leave but found we didn't really want to and stayed on — much to the management's delight. In hindsight, our presence must have meant a great deal to them in their efforts to get back to normality after their country had been so devastated by war.

Sauntering home beside the lake at 2a.m., a few of us decided that a bathe was essential. It was my first experience of "skinny dipping", and I shall never forget the exquisite sensation of cool water on a completely naked body. I remember that we were very circumspect with the men and the girls undressing in separate areas. Drying ourselves afterwards was a very superficial affair!

Next day was fairly uneventful, with Margaret and me hitching a lift into Riva with a charming Italian man, to play tennis. We enjoyed it so much that we both decided to join tennis clubs when we got back to Oxford. That night, there was live music at the Paradiso, and Chris insisted upon taking a turn on the drums. He was surprisingly good. Greatly daring, I asked if I could have a go too, and after a quick lesson, the obliging drummer allowed me to. I enjoyed it enormously and was assured by a kind — and rather drunk — audience that it didn't sound too bad, either. Once again, we bathed on the way back to the hotel.

The next day was pure magic. Again, we were rowed across the lake but then walked up through narrow lanes where wild cyclamen grew in the walls, to Lago di Ledro, another, much smaller lake nestling among the mountains. Here, there was lush vegetation threaded with little streams and waterfalls and the lake was an incredibly deep blue, streaked with turquoise along the shore line. There were huge butterflies that I have recorded as "flying backwards". I have also recorded eating enormous and delicious cream cakes in a lakeside café. I have never visited Lago de Ledro again, but I hope it is still as beautiful and unspoiled as it was then.

That night, Chris really did send the record of "That's Why The Lady Is A Tramp" skimming into the lake! And was thoroughly disconcerted when the management immediately produced another!

Next day, a fleet of cars took us on a day trip up into the Dolomites. Margaret and I, Andy, Eric and Ian all shared an ancient Fiat which headed the procession of three cars. This was just as well since it broke down on several occasions and caused us to be decanted on to the roadside while much tinkering and shouting went on. We quite enjoyed this as it meant we could inhale great gulps of the incredibly pure mountain air. At last I understood the true meaning of the phrase so beloved of writers — "the air tasted like wine". It really did.

At last, we reached our destination — the lakeside town of Molvano, which I described in my diary as "very beautiful but rather ritzy". Glass blowing was the local industry, and the gift shops, of which there were many, were full of delicate little glass animals and *objets d'art*. Andy and I drank vermouth, to which I now seemed to be addicted. The return journey was, of course, downhill and managed without incident. No-one stayed long at the Paradiso that night, the mountain air had tired us out.

We all felt rather sad next day as it was our last, and Chris decided to cheer us up by announcing that we would hold a boat race that afternoon. In the morning, Andy and I wandered up the mountain behind the hotel until we had a magnificent view over the lake and sat and gazed at it, trying to imprint it on our "inward eye". Andy told me that he and Ian and Eric would be breaking their journey home by spending a few days in Paris and suggested that I join them. They had already booked themselves in at a little *pension* on the Left Bank, but he was sure there would be no problem if I arrived as well.

Dutiful little civil servant that I was, I told him, regretfully, that I couldn't, much as I would love to, as I was due back in the office on Monday morning. But Andy would have none of it. "Send them a card," he suggested airily. "I'm sure they'll understand."

But I was just as certain that they wouldn't. In those days — I've no idea what it's like now — one simply didn't do that sort of thing. Applications for leave had to be signed and then countersigned.

"We'd have a wonderful time," Andy tempted. "Think of it. Montmartre, Notre Dame, the Rue de la Paix."

I thought — and succumbed. If I sent off a card straight away and enclosed it in an envelope to make it look more official, surely it would arrive in the office by Monday morning. And I would, without fail, be in on Tuesday morning. That would give me two glorious days in Paris. "All right!" I said, feeling as depraved as if I'd been caught drug smuggling.

But we still had most of our last day to enjoy. After the inevitable group photograph had been taken outside the Paradiso, Chris organized the boat race. Naturally, it was Oxford versus Cambridge. Being small, I was elected to be cox of the Oxford boat. Once I'd had my duties explained to me, I quite enjoyed shrieking out "One, two! One, two!" at the top of my voice, and we were soon way ahead of Cambridge. The only problem was that I was also supposed to be steering but was so carried away by the sound of my own voice that I forgot all about it. The result was that we were soon heading, very fast, for the opposite shore and in danger of being very late, indeed, for dinner! However, Chris, who had sensibly decided to conduct operations from the shore with the aid of a megaphone, and while we were still within hailing distance, declared the race to be a draw. It was a diplomatic, if not very accurate, decision, and we all retired to the bar with our dignity maintained.

We had an early start next day as we had to be up at five to catch an early train from Desenzano, en route to Venice where we were to stay overnight. Andy and I had one last vermouth together, at a little lakeside café in Torbole, and then joined the rest of the party for a riotous last night at the Paradiso. In the end, it seemed hardly worth our while to go to bed at all, and it was a very weary party who bade a tearful farewell to Chris after our early breakfast. I think that he, too, was sad to see us go.

The journey up to Venice was very hot and uncomfortable, and we dozed for most of the way. But the sight of Venice revived us and after booking in at our hotel, we embarked upon a hectic round of sightseeing. We navigated the Grand Canal on a steamer, drank the most expensive coffee of our lives in St. Mark's Square, fed the already overfed pigeons and cricked our necks gazing up at countless frescoes. Andy

184

and I finished off with a romantic ride in a gondola with the gondolier regaling us with appropriate Italian love songs. At least, I assume they were appropriate; he could have been entertaining us with vitriolic, anti-British propaganda for all we knew! But anyway, it sounded great, and we were, by then, almost asleep on our feet. It was all highly satisfactory, and I went to bed in a state of happy exhaustion and with Paris still to look forward to.

I couldn't have slept for that long because my diary tells me that we left for Paris at 6a.m., changing at Turin and Milan and spending the night, most uncomfortably, on the train. We arrived in Paris at half past seven and then it was off to the Pension des Familles with Andy, Eric and Ian and feeling very emancipated as we waved goodbye to the rest of the party. I had, of course, arranged to see Margaret soon after I got back to Oxford.

The Pension des Familles could have come out of a Somerset Maugham novel. I remember a spiral staircase — up which I fell on a couple of painful occasions! — and a dining room with one enormous table around which everyone sat *en famille* and with "Madame, la proprietare" presiding. We were all expected to speak French, so I doubt if we English said very much. However, the only meal we were expected to be in for was breakfast, and this was highly satisfactory with enormous bowls of coffee and chunks of bread to dunk in it. There was no butter but, as we were paying a miniscule amount, this wasn't expected. The table was covered by a sort of flowered linoleum which must have been very easy to wipe down. We dunked happily and slurped as noisily as any of the French residents around us.

After breakfast, we were ready for yet another day of sightseeing and managed to visit the Rue de la Paix, the Tuileries, the Champs Elysee and the Arc de Triomphe. "Very weary!" my diary records.

Next day, it was Notre Dame and a trip out to Versailles where Andy and I spent more time wandering in the gardens, hand in hand, than in the actual palace. That evening, we all went to the Folies Bergere. I've no idea if medical students find nude, female models more or less alluring than other people, and I didn't ask! But I think we all felt we could now cross one more item off our list of Parisian "must-do's".

The next day, Andy and I spent entirely on our own. Again we wandered around Notre Dame, but this time we climbed to the top and were rewarded by a wonderful view over Paris. Before we left, we lit candles in front of the Virgin Mary. Why, I'm not quite sure, but it seemed the appropriate thing to do. Then we joined the Sunday morning crowds strolling beside the river and dawdling among the second hand bookstalls.

Next morning, Andy saw me off at the Gare St. Lazare after an emotional farewell, although we had arranged to meet when were both back in England. My diary records "good crossing, although choppy". I eventually reached Oxford at two o'clock in the morning. There is no record of how I got back into the YWCA at that hour!

CHAPTER
TWENTY-TWO

The only downside to having such a wonderful holiday is that no holiday since then has ever quite measured up to it. Never again did I end up in Paris with three medical students and have the time of my life! Mind you, my return to the office was not all open arms and welcoming words. In the Civil Service, I was informed, one did not send postcards from abroad asking for an extension to one's leave, even if only for a day. One submitted one's application so many days beforehand and it might, or might not, be approved. All this, I had known perfectly well, of course, but had also known that, presented with a *fait accompli*, there was little they could do about it. And to get sacked from the Civil Service one had to commit some heinous crime like murdering one's grandmother. But I was also aware that I was taking advantage of my boss's good nature. Of course, I promised never to do such a thing again, and all was forgiven, and I settled down to telling everyone about my holiday and enjoying the rest of the summer.

The Civil Service, I was delighted to discover, was allowed to use the courts and facilities of a local tennis club and among the players was a youngish and very amusing University lecturer called Freddie from the north of England. I wasn't in the least attracted to him physically but found him very good company and — he had a car! When he invited me out one Sunday for a trip to the seaside, I accepted with alacrity but also hedged my bets, as it were, by asking my old hostel friend, Joyce to come with us. With appalling lack of courtesy, I deliberately neglected to tell Freddie what I had done. Such behaviour would have caused most guys to not only call the whole trip off but also to kill any further interest he might have in me. But Freddie was made of sterner stuff. After an initial protest, he gave in gracefully and we all had a most enjoyable day. After that, a threesome became quite a regular thing.

I continued to see Margaret on a regular basis, but many of her evenings and weekends were spent at another tennis club — and where, I am delighted to say, she met the man of her dreams.

Bob was a tea planter, home from Assam on a long leave. Tall, blonde and in his early forties, he and Margaret took an immediate shine to each other and, since his time in this country was limited, saw each other on every possible occasion. Within days, it seemed, he was asking her to marry him, and she was accepting.

Meanwhile, "back at the ranch", so to speak, events were moving for me, too. While there was no prescribed upper age limit for residents at the hostel, I was several years older than most of the others and while this hadn't bothered the elderly warden who was in charge when I arrived, a change of management had meant she was replaced by a slightly younger warden with a keen eye for discipline.

On reflection, she must have considered me to be a bad influence on the others for, upon finding me cleaning my teeth in the bathroom at 11.30p.m. when "lights out" was at eleven, she immediately suggested in a no-argument sort of voice, that it might be an idea if I found accommodation elsewhere. She wasn't exactly giving me notice, but the writing was on the wall.

It was round about that time that David unexpectedly invited me to a dance at his college. He wasn't inviting me as his particular partner — although my mother did get very excited when I told her about it — but as one of a party that he was first taking out to dinner at a nearby restaurant.

All my young hostel friends shared my sense of anticipation and slight apprehension and immediately set to work to make me as presentable as possible. Our main preoccupation, of course, was deciding what I should wear. It was then that the benefits of living in a hostel really showed. In the end, I went off for the evening in a very pretty, short taffeta dress, that belonged to Jill but fitted me well. Around my neck, I wore a black velvet ribbon, choker style, with a cameo pinned to it, courtesy of Joyce. And over this finery, I wore a lacy, cream shawl belonging to Jean. In my hand, I clutched an evening bag lent to me by Mary. My shoes were my own!

I reached the designated restaurant on a bus — a taxi would have been far too expensive. In Swansea, no-one would have caught a bus if they were wearing a long dress, but in post-war Oxford, you could get away with anything. I once saw a young male undergraduate using his bicycle as a one-man removal business. On his head, he wore a lampshade, conical in shape, around his neck, the flex of the lamp and, tied to his handlebars, the lamp itself. Strapped to his crossbar were several cushions and behind his saddle was a box, piled high with books. And in spite of the Saturday afternoon traffic on Carfax, he was still managing to ride it, albeit a trifle precariously. I remember smiling broadly at this Heath Robinson affair and he, catching my eye, smiled, even more broadly back. I also remember thinking what a pity it was that I couldn't just follow him to wherever he was going because he looked such a nice guy!

But back to David's dance. I had a good time! Included in the party was an old school friend of David's who had recently broken up with his fiancée; a fact I discovered when we strolled down to Magdalen Bridge soon after dawn broke. In return, I explained that I was David's "ex". In hindsight, it may have been David's kind intention to bring us together to see if we "gelled", but nothing came of it. Also in the party were his younger brother and a very pleasant Norwegian woman who seemed to be an old family friend. They took me back to the hostel in their car at about 5a.m., and I remember that David's friend, with superb good manners, crunched across the gravel and punctiliously waited at the open window of Joyce's basement room until I had made a soft landing on her bed and signalled that all was well. He could have been

190

delivering me to the pillared portico of some country mansion! I suppose the evening was most memorable for showing me that I had definitely "got over" David. I hadn't minded at all that his chosen partner for the evening had been the girl I had seen him with on the river the day after we had stopped seeing each other. My weekend in Paris had been therapeutic as well as romantic!

In view of the warden's hostility, I had started looking out for a bedsit in the North Oxford area and soon found one that Sasha, another hostel friend and I, decided to share. Besides our room, we were allowed to use the dining room by pre-arrangement with the other residents and, greatly daring, I decided to ask Margaret and Bob to supper. I say "greatly daring" because I had never entertained before.

My diary records that we dined on grapefruit, followed by spaghetti and scrambled egg on toast, followed by cheese and biscuits, coffee and Aurum liqueur (brought back from Italy) and cake. A varied feast, indeed, and Margaret and Bob were profuse in their appreciation, but in their euphoric state, they would probably have been just as enthusiastic about bread and jam!

My diary also records a weekend that Sasha and I spent in Cambridge meeting up with Andy, Ian and Eric. We stayed at a guesthouse called The Hermitage — "full of old ladies", I have recorded somewhat disparagingly — and met the lads in Andy's rooms in Queens. The *piece de resistance* was listening to the recording of Paloma Bianca, which Andy had bought in

Verona. On Sunday, we were taken on the river and discovered that it was the practice at Cambridge to pole from the opposite end of the punt to Oxford! It was a very pleasant weekend but Andy and I decided that it would have been even better if it had been just the two of us.

Soon after this, Margaret married Bob before his leave expired and he went back to Assam. Of course, she gave up her flat. Would I like to take it on? Would I not! But what about Sasha? Having inveigled her out of the YWCA, it seemed hardly fair to abandon her, as it were, and the flat was only big enough for one.

But, very sportingly, she declared that she would be quite happy to find a smaller bedsit just for herself and that I had done her a good turn in getting her out of the YWCA where she was in danger of taking root. I hope this was true. She was a very sweet person who would have put other people's feelings before her own. Years later, I was relieved to hear that she had married and was still living in Oxford, which she loved.

Moving into the flat in Park Town, a beautifully proportioned "oval" of terraced, Georgian houses just around the corner from the hostel was one of the happiest days of my time in Oxford. The flat was on the top floor and consisted of a bedsit with a landing outside which had been adapted into a kitchen with cupboards and a small electric cooker. Leading off the landing was a large bathroom which was virtually mine although theoretically shared with the occupant of the bedsit below me — at the time, a very pleasant female student called Hilary.

192

The main room, although on the small side, was tastefully decorated with curtains and bed cover in a very pretty *Toile de Jouy* fabric. The window looked out on to the communal garden in the centre of the oval. It was possible to stand outside the window, lean on the parapet which ran round the top of the crescent and gaze up at the sky or down on to the tree tops. I remember standing out there one night and gazing up at the stars, conscious not only of infinite space above me but also feeling quite safe and secure behind my parapet. Ever since, this has seemed to me to be the epitome of a happy life — security but also with endless possibilities stretching ahead. And I make no apologies if this sounds like "having your cake and eating it"! Why not, after all?

The rent for my flat was £2 per week and I remember feeling slightly worried at the time about whether I could really afford it, but I knew that I had to give it a go.

Naturally, I held a flat-warming party soon after I'd moved in. My guests were a pleasing mix of hostel friends and office friends and my charming landlord and landlady, who diplomatically left after one drink. The drinks were a very motley collection; I remember one bottle of sherry, a few bottles of beer plus whatever the guests brought. If a guest opted for sherry, I had to explain that, initially, only one glass would be allowed before they went on to "something else". However, once everyone had arrived, the remainder of the bottle would be "up for grabs". No-one seemed to mind this proviso. Someone, I remember, brought a bottle of something called, simply, "333" which tasted rather like cough mixture but had a delayed, but pronounced, kick-back. No-one wanted more than one glass of it!

In spite of its limitations — perhaps because of them — the party was deemed a great success, and I remember ending it sitting on the doorstep saying goodnight to a male office friend who'd arrived on a motorbike and wished to "take me for a spin" then and there. Fortunately, I persuaded him to delay it for a time until he'd sobered up and we had a very pleasant run out to Dorchester.

Soon after I had moved, Andy came to visit for the weekend, staying at a small hotel on the Banbury Road. On the Sunday, I took him out to Benson on the bus, and we spent an entertaining day walking in the Chilterns while I tried to find the exact spot where the Americans had found me, bare legged and tie-less during the war. I couldn't, so we found our own spot! In the evening, I cooked us bacon and eggs in the flat — it was wonderful having my own space.

Meanwhile, back in Swansea, my mother was growing increasingly restless. She had long had the ambition to live in an English village and preferably in a thatched cottage with the obligatory roses around the door. I had begun in a desultory sort of way, to look for one around Oxford but now that I had my own place, I suggested that she came to stay for a while and looked for herself. My landlady was quite happy with the arrangement, and we spent several nights crammed into my single bed.

She didn't find her cottage, but she did register with several estate agents which was a step in the right direction. My father was still living and working in London and was quite happy to leave the search to her. Her visit was particularly memorable because of her maiden visit to a pub — my father, of course, had never darkened their doors, at least not after they were married. After much thought, I decided on the Trout, a very attractive riverside pub in North Oxford, and Joyce and I took her there on a lovely summer's evening when we were able to sit outside and enjoy the view. We couldn't decide what we should suggest she drank; cider, which was our favourite tipple being very reasonably priced, we considered to be too potent and in the end, we opted for a sweet sherry which she enjoyed immensely. I don't know if she ever told my father — I doubt it!

Christmas came, and I went back to Swansea for a quiet but enjoyable few days. For the next few months, Oxford continued to be as enjoyable as ever, but I was slowly beginning to realise that I couldn't really afford to go on living in my flat. Two pounds a week out of my diminutive salary was too much. While discussing this in the office one day, Sydney came up with the perfect solution. Why didn't I come and live in Brill? He happened to know that there was a cottage to rent on the common for a pound a week and I could drive in every day with him and Betty.

It was the answer to my prayers. My landlord and landlady were sympathetic and understanding. They would be sorry to see me go, but they knew there would be no difficulty in re-letting the flat. So, one Saturday afternoon in June, I packed my meagre possessions into Sydney's car and moved out to Brill.

Rookery Cottage was right on the edge of the Common with a wonderful view over the countryside towards Oxford and Shotover Hill. It was the end one of what had once been a row of four old cottages, three of which had been knocked into one, where my landlord lived with his wife, leaving my cottage as a separate dwelling.

The main living room had a big, kitchen range along one wall — which I don't remember ever lighting — one big window looking out on to a field and the view to Oxford and another, smaller one looking out on to a tiny front garden, the Common and the windmill. Off the living room was a small kitchen, and two small bedrooms were reached by a winding little staircase leading off the living room. All the woodwork in the living room was painted a bright, emerald green which I always meant to paint a cool cream but again, never did. There was no bathroom as such and washing — both the dishes and me — had to be accomplished in the kitchen sink. However, and rather oddly, I was allowed a weekly bath at the Ministry in a bathroom that was, apparently, left over from the war years. So, once a week, I would take a towel and sponge bag — and a bottle of Dettol — into work. It was rather like being back in the WAAF! My toilet requirements were taken care of by an Elsan situated in a little hut in the garden, next to the coal shed. More of that later.

The cottage was let furnished, and I particularly remember a big, round table in the middle of the living room and, against one wall, a large, glass-fronted china cabinet in which I had, as yet, nothing to display. One capacious armchair stood near the range, alongside three upright dining chairs. Upstairs, there was a single bed in each room and a chair. A curtain across one corner of the larger room improvised as a wardrobe. The smaller room had a chest of drawers. The window in the larger bedroom looked out towards Oxford and was so low, I could lie in bed and gaze out at the fields, usually occupied by sheep. The mattresses, I remember, were rather hard, and one of them was stuffed with straw and crackled when I turned over, but it was surprisingly comfortable.

Tired after the move, I slept like a log on my first night but — my diary records — was awakened at 4.30a.m. by the sound of sheep bleating and again at 5.30a.m. by cows moo-ing. "So much for the peace of the countryside!" I have written. But I loved it. My overwhelming memory is of the glorious summer scents floating in through the open windows. That first weekend, I picked a great armful of buttercups, clover — pink and white — moon daisies, honeysuckle and meadowsweet and arranged them in a huge, china bowl. They didn't last long, of course but looked and smelled good for a couple of days. The previous occupant had planted wall-flowers in the garden beneath the front window and their fragrance when the sun shone on them was heavenly. I certainly felt very blessed on that first weekend, especially since the

Rosendales very kindly invited me to an enormous Sunday lunch, prepared by Sydney, who was an excellent cook.

The pattern of the days was soon established. Each working day, I would walk up into the village to the Rosendales where I would climb into the back seat of the Bentley for a somewhat windy but exhilarating drive to work. It was possible to pull up a cover over the seats but this was only done in exceptionally rainy weather. I don't remember it ever happening when I was on board. Most days, we had to wear scarves and sometimes, woolly ski caps.

On Saturdays — the Civil Service still worked on Saturday mornings until midday — a local village firm ran a bus that came back to Brill in the afternoon, which I used to catch, usually laden with groceries. My main midday meal was eaten in the excellent office canteen, and I usually had a snack supper; cheese on toast was one of my specialities. Sunday lunch was usually chops or a stew with a basis of tinned meat. I never remember being ill when I was in the cottage, so my diet must have been reasonably healthy.

Every Monday evening, my landlord would call in for the rent and enter it in an official-looking rent book which made me feel very grown up. Sometimes, at weekends, they would invite me in for tea. I once reciprocated and was determined to make a cake — the first in my life. Unfortunately, it turned out a soggy mess, and I was reduced to opening a packet of biscuits. The cake, I turned into a rather revolting pudding which I ate next day with a tin of custard.

Apart from this sad occurrence, life in the country, I decided, was idyllic. In fact, it was too idyllic to last. Suddenly, everything changed when Sydney left the Ministry of Ag., Fish and Food and moved to a more lucrative job, much nearer home, at a nearby army depot. From then on, my methods of getting into work were many and varied. Betty, more often than not, stayed with a friend in Oxford during the week.

Most importantly, Sydney introduced me to a nice young guy, not long out of the army, who drove into the lovely old market town of Thame each morning to his work in a garage and was happy to take me in with him. From Thame, I could get a bus into Oxford. Interestingly, Tony's mother, a widow, ran the Brill telephone exchange; this meant that the actual apparatus — a sizeable affair not unlike a junior Enigma, code-breaking machine — took pride of place in their living room and was with them, a sort of lurking presence, twenty-four hours a day. This meant that Tony's Mum would regularly have to stop what she was doing — be it dusting the furniture, cooking the dinner or having a nap — and connect callers either to each other or to the outside world. Presumably, when she had to attend to "the calls of nature", as it was called, the subscriber had to wait.

Another method of getting to work was to cycle. If it was a lovely summer's morning, it was very pleasant indeed, and I would whiz along through the villages of Horton-cum-Studley and Stanton St. John, singing at the top of my voice. Once when I was cycling home, quite late in the evening, beside a patch of woodland, I heard the nightingale for the first time — it was magical.

Once, when Tony was having a day off, and my cycle was off the road with a flat tyre, I had to hitch to work. It was a hazardous business since there was very little traffic on those cross-country roads, and I was extremely grateful when a tractor drew up beside me. He could only take me a couple of miles and at a snail's pace, but it did mean I reached work on time. Most of my hostel friends were now living in bedsits in Oxford and were quite happy to let me doss down on their floor, curled up in my sleeping bag. One way or another, I was never late for work, and it was all worth it for the pleasure of living in the country.

Friends from Oxford would often come for the weekend. Freddy drove out on several occasions, usually bringing Joyce with him — which leads me, by somewhat devious means, into the story of my Elsan, or Ellie as I had christened it.

As I've already said, it lived in a shed in the garden. If you didn't own a flush toilet — and lots of country dwellers didn't — you usually resorted to an Elsan, which was considered to be one up on the old bucket earth closet at the bottom of the garden. It consisted of a large, round, metal cylinder with a removable lining and topped with a conventional toilet seat. Into the cylinder you poured a couple of inches of some chemical fluid which was guaranteed to make it smell, if not like roses, then certainly not like it normally would.

The problems created by the necessity of emptying the cylinder's lining meant I became adept at "going" elsewhere; either at a friend's or, if cycling home in the dark, behind a hedge; anything to delay having to dig a hole in the garden! However, that first summer, I did grow some exceptionally robust tomatoes, and I feel confident it was down to Ellie. A few years back, I was told by the locals, when nearly all the village had had earth closets, a horse and cart would tour the village in the dead of night, collecting buckets and emptying them, presumably in some massive pit somewhere in the countryside. The driver, I was told in all seriousness, was called Dan, the dirty old man!

However, when my mother, still in search of her dream cottage, came to stay for a couple of weeks, everything changed. Left to her own devices during the day, unless she had come into Oxford with me, she discovered while doing some weeding that the Water Board had placed a manhole cover in one corner of the tiny patch of grass grandly referred to as "the lawn". Prising this up with the aid of a large garden fork, she discovered a sort of subterranean cavern containing some dark liquid, presumably water, and, without more ado, poured in the current contents of the Elsan. Problem solved! And with no dire consequences since our tap water continued to run crystal clear.

Thereafter, not being nearly as tough and well-muscled as my mother, whenever anyone of the opposite sex came to visit, I would, before their departure, inveigle them into Emptying Ellie! Freddy, naturally, was no exception so, one Sunday evening before his and Joyce's departure for Oxford, he obligingly went out into the dusk, armed with the garden fork. Five minutes later, he was back, limping, white-faced and clutching his groin. Apparently — and he'd never mentioned it before — he had a hernia which had "popped out", as he put it, when subjected to the strain of heaving up the manhole cover. Panic stations! Clearly, he needed medical care but regrettably, I knew nothing of Brill's capacity to provide it. Praying that they would be at home, I set off across the common with a torch in search of Sydney and Betty. I found them enjoying a quiet evening at home but immediately and with the cooperation of Tony's Mum in her front room, telephoned a local doctor. He, complete with little black bag, arrived at the cottage almost as quickly as me.

While Joyce and I lurked in the kitchen, Freddy was examined in the living room and, after some sort of manipulation on the doctor's part, was declared to be as fit as he'd ever be although advised a) to see his own doctor as soon as possible and b) not to heave up any more manhole covers in a hurry! He, the doctor, was clearly greatly amused by the whole event. Before departing into the night, he added that it might be as well if Freddy didn't drive until the next morning. So, I thought philosophically as I rummaged for clean sheets, I was at least assured of a lift in the morning!

Andy also came to stay for a weekend and I — a sign of the moral atmosphere of the times — in order not to shock the landlord, went to stay at Sydney's for the night, leaving Andy to sleep on his own in the cottage.

I remember thinking how hypocritical it all was since it didn't, apparently, matter what shenanigans we got up to during the hours of daylight when we were there on our own! Anyway, it didn't spoil our weekend which we seem to have spent either walking or in the Plough — a lovely little pub in the village, where you sat on benches against the wall in what had clearly once been someone's living room, and Jim Hone, the landlord, a tiny, charming man who always wore a brown overall, had to go down several steps into the cellar to draw a pint of beer because that was where the pumps were. He claimed the exercise kept him fit, and the customers could always be sure of having really cold beer. It came as no surprise when, upon Jim's death several years later, the pub reverted to being a private house, and antiques were sold in the erstwhile cellar.

Bit by bit, I was adding to my meagre possessions. Sydney gave me an old Toby jug that he would have thrown out if I hadn't spotted it and threw in a couple of very pretty plates whose cracks, as far as I was concerned, didn't diminish their beauty and looked good displayed on my cottage wall.

However, these acquisitions were purely cosmetic. My sensible ones came from my parents who came to occupy the cottage on their summer holidays while I went off on mine. They consisted of a three bar electric fire which would be invaluable in the winter months and a reliable alarm clock which meant that from then on, if I was getting a lift from someone in the village, other than kind Tony who would always wait, I would arrive in good time and not have to go haring down the village street, shouting at the top of my voice as had happened on a couple of occasions. I was rapidly acquiring the reputation as "that strange girl who lives on the Common and is never on time!"

But one precious acquisition I made that summer, I bought myself. If I'd had a lift into Thame with Tony, he would always deposit me at the Oxford bus stop, which was in the centre of the town, outside an antique shop called The Witchball. Waiting there one morning with Betty, I noticed in the window an arrangement of five, dark green wine goblets which I immediately knew I had to have. For some time, fostered by gazing at a collection of ruby and green glassware that Betty and Sydney had arranged in their cottage, I had longed to own some myself. Here was the opportunity, because the glasses in the window were priced at only one pound.

"That," said Betty shrewdly, "is because there are only five. If there were the customary six, they would be worth a lot more."

But I couldn't have cared less that there were only five. I had no intention of actually using them — I just wanted to put them in my recently acquired china cabinet and admire them — and I could just about afford a pound. I still have them, now occupying pride of place in my corner cupboard.

I never remember it raining that summer of 1949 and, in fact, it must have been pretty hot because my diary records skinny dipping in the Thames late one night, with Joyce and Freddy at Sandford Lock near Oxford. I certainly remember it being icy cold —

considerably cooler than I remembered Lake Garda! Which brings me, neatly, I hope, to my holiday that year.

Joyce and I had decided that we would go to France. Travelling independently and not on a package deal, we would go, by rail and cross-channel steamer, to Paris and from there hitch south, hopefully as far as the Mediterranean where we would stay for a few days. We might even, if funds and time permitted, cross it to reach Tunisia where I wanted to visit Bill's grave.

Surprisingly, apart from the last leg, things went more or less to plan. At the beginning of September, we caught the train to Newhaven where Andy, home on a long vacation, met us in his father's car and drove us up to Beachy Head before seeing us on to the ferry. Arriving in Paris at 6a.m., we went immediately to the Hotel de la Vigne — not where I'd stayed in the previous summer but also on the Left Bank — where we'd booked a room and went straight to bed. Waking about midday, refreshed but hungry, we emerged into the Paris sunshine and lunched on *bifsteak* and *pommes frites* at the nearby Polydor restaurant. Then began the exhausting but exhilarating process of introducing Joyce to Paris, although, on that first day, we seemed to have restricted ourselves to the Pantheon and the Luxembourg Gardens before having an early night.

Next day, however, we more than made up for it; Place de l'Opera, my diary records, Rue de la Paix, the Tuileries, a Gauguin exhibition at l'Orangerie and an evening visit to the Opera House to hear *Samson and*

Delilah. I write "hear", since we didn't exactly see any of it. That morning, we had considered ourselves very lucky indeed to be able to get tickets for the evening performance without having to pay the earth for them. Admittedly, along with the tickets had come a torrent of French that had gone right over our heads, but we nodded wisely as if we understood every word. Now we understood what the girl in the ticket bureau had been trying to tell us! For, presenting ourselves at the Opera House at the appointed time, we were indeed shown into a box or, at the least the first part of it. Sadly, I'm still not familiar with boxes in the major Opera Houses of the world, so I don't know how usual it is for them to have a sort of little foyer through which you pass before reaching the part that looks over the stage, but certainly the Paris Opera House had them — or had them at that time. In this foyer, chairs had been placed where we were to sit for the entire performance. Admittedly, if we had been devoted opera lovers, this would probably have been enough — many people listen to music with their eyes shut anyway — but we were not, and I'm afraid we didn't last the course. We emerged into the Paris night after the first act. However, we were allowed one enticing glimpse of the stage before we went by kind permission of the privileged people seated in the front of the box, and we did at least enjoy the magnificence of the actual building.

Needless to say, we didn't go straight back to our hotel but sought consolation at a pavement café on the Rue Saint Michel. There, over a couple of cold beers, we met a charming American student called Bruce. I remember, as the beer hit its mark, trying to hold an intelligent conversation with him about existentialism and Jean Paul Sartre, about which I would have had only the scantiest of knowledge. However, Bruce didn't seem to notice — perhaps he didn't know much about them either — and insisted upon seeing us back to our hotel, only leaving us after we had arranged to meet for coffee next morning at the same café. Feeling rather pleased with ourselves — our very own "American in Paris"! — we fell into bed and a beer-induced slumber. Sadly, as a result, we both overslept next morning and never saw him again. Another "might have been"? Who knows?

Anyway, it doesn't seem to have cramped our style, as we acquired yet another escort the next day. This one was very English and called Dennis, and all I remember about him now was that he wore a Trilby hat pulled, rather rakishly, over one eye and that he had twinkly blue eyes. We met him, perhaps appropriately, at the Folies Bergere where we went the next evening and sat next to him. Having an escort made all the difference to our Parisian night life as after supper — which Dennis insisted upon paying for — we all went to Les Hailes, followed by a memorable visit to the Sacre Coeur. I shall never forget standing on its steps and gazing out at the lights of Paris shining below us. Again at Dennis's expense — he seemed to have an unlimited cash flow — we went back to our respective hotels in a taxi. Dennis's, I remember, was considerably smarter than ours. Again, we made plans to meet up the next day — and this time, we made it and had a very enjoyable dinner with him in Montpamasse. By now, Joyce and I felt like seasoned Parisiennes but, sadly, we were due to leave the next day. Saying goodbye to Dennis was sad, too, but we'd all enjoyed our time together, and we all knew there was no way he was going to stand on the side of the road and use his thumb!

Next morning, with, for us, surprising common sense, we took the Metro out to the edge of the city to the busy main road south towards Lyons and stood hopefully on the verge, rucksacks at our feet, thumbs well elevated and optimistic smiles on our faces. We hadn't long to wait. An obliging lorry driver squealed to a stop and up we climbed into his cabin. We were on our way!

Somewhere — it might have been at Nevers — we had a comfort stop and a quick cup of coffee and began to walk back towards "our" lorry. There, our driver had had what I at first considered to be a brilliant idea; he had been talking to a mate who was going the same way as us. Since it was obviously going to be a very hot day why, he asked with deceptive innocence, didn't we travel in comfort with one of us going with his friend and the other staying with himself?

"What a good . . ." I began but was silenced by a sharp kick on the ankle from Joyce.

"No," she said firmly, "we stay together or we leave you here."

Sadly, we left him there! But she was so right. Even after four years in the WAAF — where, some cynics declared, we were there solely for the pleasure of the male personnel — I was still as green as I was cabbage

208

looking, as the saying goes — while Joyce, at least three years my junior, hadn't a fleck of green in her make-up.

Anyway, the long and short of it was that we were once more back on the roadside and, to begin with, without result. We'd even begun to discuss the times of trains and buses when another lorry drew up, this time with an older driver who was going as far as Clermont Ferrand. To us, Clermont Ferrand sounded as good as anywhere, and we would soon have to find somewhere to stay for the night. However, Clermont, set so beautifully among the mountains looked far too inviting for only one night's stay, so we found a small hotel and booked in for two. Next morning, we shopped in the market for cheese, bread and tomatoes and picnicked a couple of miles out of Clermont, near the towering Puy de Dome with its huge cross at its summit. It was a good day.

I can't remember what we had for dinner that night — perhaps something different from our customary *bif-steak* and *pommes frites* — but whatever it was, it caused Joyce to be violently sick all night. There was no way we could continue on our way the next day. Somewhat grudgingly — for she obviously feared Joyce was suffering from something long and contagious — our landlady agreed that we could stay another night.

While Joyce stayed in bed, I "did" Clermont and, to everyone's great relief, in the late afternoon Joyce said she felt much better. However, a day of convalescence seemed a good idea and, our landlady being by now quite amenable, we booked in for another night. At least half of Joyce's convalescence was spent in the cinema watching *The Road to Zanzibar*, which we had mistakenly thought would be in English with French subtitles instead of the other way round. However, it was quite enjoyable, and Joyce slept through most of it, anyway.

Early next morning and after bidding a, by now, quite affectionate farewell to our landlady, we started walking through the beautiful countryside of the Auvergne in the direction of the main road south. With the help of an obliging farmer driving to Lyons, we made it by midday and took up position just south of the city. By now, we were resigned to a succession of lorry drivers and could hardly believe our luck when a car drew up beside us — and not any old car. This one was large and luxurious and driven by one of the kindest men I've ever met. He'd been on a business trip to Paris and was returning to Nice where he lived with his family, and he would be delighted he assured us, to have our company. We began to think we were doing him a favour! Once our rucksacks had been piled into the boot, we settled into our seats — Joyce in the back where she immediately went to sleep and me next to the driver; the only downside was that he spoke no English so that I had to keep up a conversation in my schoolgirl French. But, it was well worth it as we glided south down the Rhone Valley.

It was his custom, our new friend explained, to stay overnight in Valence during his trips and, to this end, had already booked a room there. What did we want to do? It was quite a large hotel, and he was sure there would be a room there for us if we so wished. However, we might like to stay elsewhere? He must have known that our finances were limited. However, we were terrified of "losing" him in some way so decided to stay at the hotel but to have our supper elsewhere. I did my best to explain to Paul that we hadn't the right clothes for a smart dining room — which was true — and he said he quite understood. Assuring us that he would see us at breakfast — the price for this was included in our stay — we parted at the reception desk. So we had our inexpensive meal somewhere in the back streets but did enjoy wonderful hot baths in the hotel afterwards.

Next day, having clearly given the matter some thought, our friend said he thought it would be to our advantage to stay somewhere just outside Nice rather than in Nice itself. He knew of a nice little hotel in Cap St. Jean Ferrat that he thought would suit us very well. This we readily agreed to and then gave ourselves up to enjoying France as we sped through it far too quickly but with a running commentary from our host who clearly loved his country.

I remember Montelimar, given over to the manufacture of nougat, Nimes, later to become the origin of the word "denim" and Aix en Provence where we stopped for coffee at a café in the tree-lined main street. The countryside, I managed to comment to our friend, looked exactly as it did in the paintings of Van Gogh. Hardly surprising, of course, but it clearly pleased him to hear that I knew of Van Gogh's work, and he launched into a eulogy of the painter. The coast road along the shores of the Mediterranean was a revelation. The resorts must still have been recovering from the effects of the war years, but nothing could take away the beauty of the sea on the one hand and the mountains on the other. Our driver gave us a dissertation upon the village of Grasse, high above us and famous for its fields of flowers and the perfume distilled from them.

"You must come back another day," he told me, "and climb up to it on the back of a donkey. That's the right way to see it and to smell it."

He also showed us the turning down to Lavendou, a quiet little Mediterranean fishing village. "Go before it gets spoiled," he urged. I haven't been, but perhaps it hasn't been spoiled either.

It was a tired but supremely grateful couple of Brits that he eventually deposited in Cap Ferrat and presented his card to. He and his wife, he assured us, would always be delighted to see us. We felt quite bereft as he drove off into the gathering dusk, having first made sure that the hotel he recommended could accommodate us.

Not only did the hotel — called La Freigate — accommodate us, it gave us a room with a wonderful view from where, throughout our stay, we would lie in bed and watch the sunrise — a magical experience. The hotel specialized in serving fish so fresh it was barely out of the sea.

Next day, at my insistence, we took a bus into Nice for the specific purpose of booking our return trip to Paris on a coach. When I thought about the mileage we had covered and the hazards we had experienced, I knew there was no way I was going to trust to hitching for the return journey. Joyce was in between jobs so wasn't worried over how long it would take to get home, but I knew I couldn't risk a repeat of the previous year when I'd gone AWOL even though it meant using up some of our precious reserves. We were lucky that the coach would take us through Grenoble and the French Alps to Lyons, thus showing us even more of the French countryside.

My mind now at rest, we set about enjoying our stay in Cap Ferrat. It was, we were to discover, one of the most beautiful, and therefore the most select parts of the Cote d'Azur. Somerset Maugham, we were told, had a villa nearby, hidden among trees and completely invisible from the road. But we didn't begrudge it to him. We were more than happy with the small public beach since the tourists had long gone, and we had it almost to ourselves. Greatly daring, for neither of us could really swim, we sometimes hired a Pedallo and pedalled far out into the bay. It was wonderfully relaxing to lie back, occasionally rotating our feet and soak up the sun with no dangerous currents to worry about and the wonderful coastline to gaze back on. Afterwards, we would take a picnic up on to the cliffs and marvel at the view from a different perspective.

Judging by my diary, we seem to have also made a habit of dropping into "La Paloma", a sort of café cum wine bar but with facilities, and where we often played table tennis with the local lads. Once again, we went into Nice and had a meal at a place called Charlie's, where we met some sailors off *HMS Liverpool*, anchored just up the coast at Villefranche. There was going to be a dance in Villefranche on Sunday, they informed us, so why didn't we walk over and join them? This we promised to do — and did. But there were so many sailors there, and, at first glance, all identical in their uniform, we never found "our" sailors. Not that it mattered — we had a very good time.

Next day, we had to catch our coach to Grenoble, on the first leg of our journey to Paris. The scenery, I remember, was breathtaking, and the mountain air, when we stopped high in the Alps for coffee, was reminiscent of the Dolomites. We breathed in great gulps of it and were amused to find a charming, middle-aged English woman doing the same. Apparently, she quite often did the journey as she had a flat in Nice as well as one in Paris. Before we reached Grenoble, she told us of a good, but cheap, hotel there where she had stayed when she had had to "count her francs". She now stayed in a more expensive one and insisted upon taking us out for a meal when the coach reached Grenoble.

Next morning, we only just remembered in the nick of time, that we had left our passports under our mattresses. Why under our mattresses? I don't quite know! I do remember being warned that we must never, ever, be parted from them when we were hitching, for losing one, or having it stolen, was a very serious offence — it may even have been criminal. There was always the fear, one must suppose, albeit a remote one, that someone might creep into our room at night while we were asleep and try to steal them. So — we slept on them! Very commendable but only if you remembered to retrieve them the next morning! Which we only did because our new friend asked us if we had them when we met her at the coach station. And it's lucky she did; I would most certainly have been late back to the office — probably by several days!

We had to stay overnight in Paris but, luckily, were able to stay at our previous hotel and crossed to Newhaven next day, eventually arriving in Oxford via Victoria Coach Station. There, Freddy met us and drove us out to the cottage where Joyce was to stay until she started her next job. It was the end of another memorable holiday, and I was soon thinking about the next. Tunisia? Norway? Italy, again? Or what about skiing in Austria? In those heady, post-war days, even though cheap air travel was still to come, the world was my oyster.

But before that, there was my first winter at the cottage to experience. Having said that, I seem to have spent a lot of it in Oxford on "sleepovers" as my grandchildren would now describe them.

Sadly, Joyce had decided to leave Oxford and return to her home town of Birmingham for a while, but all my other hostel friends were now living in bedsits in Oxford and were quite happy to have me bedding down on their settees — or their floors! — in my sleeping bag. Barbara was now very friendly, and heading towards matrimony, with an undergraduate called James who lived in rooms in New Inn Hall Street and, again, was quite amenable to my occupation of his settee if I was going to the theatre or a cinema.

The Oxford Playhouse on Beaumont Street had an excellent repertory company who performed a different play each week, and I have recorded seeing Sybil Thorndyke and Lewis Casson in *Treasure Hunt* at the New Theatre. There were many others.

My old WAAF friend, Heather, was now living in Harrow with husband Dennis and first-born, Tony, and often invited me for the weekend. As did Gladys and Leonard in South Norwood and now with two children, Heather and Valerie.

But I was not without my country pursuits, one of them being horse riding. Our local coalman, Mr Gray, was married to our post lady, and they had two daughters named Pearl and Ruby. At some point, Mr Gray became automated, as it were, and exchanged his horse and cart for a lorry. But he kept the horse for his children to ride and also acquired a retired circus pony, a piebald called Patches. Having heard that I was a rider of sorts, he very kindly allowed me to ride Patches when neither of his daughters wanted him.

"Retired" was certainly the word to describe Patches and his attitude towards his new life. Clearly, in his opinion, he'd done his stuff in the ring and, while he had no objection to plodding sedately along the lanes, he certainly wasn't going to go any faster. No amount of drumming my heels on his sides made the slightest difference. Until, one day when I was leading him back to his field on a head collar having left his tack at the Grays, the sound of a lawn mower wafted over the Common as someone gave their grass its final cut of the year. Patches's reaction was immediate and, for a

216

moment, quite terrifying. Rearing up on to his hind legs into a posture that would have done credit to a Lippizaner mare in the Spanish Riding School in Vienna or a charger on the battlefields of Waterloo, he pawed the air with his front legs and shook his head violently from side to side before descending smartly to the ground and starting the whole process once again. This went on for about five minutes while I held on to his head collar for dear life and thanked heaven that at least I hadn't been on his back — because I would certainly have ended up flat on mine. But when he finally came down to earth and proceeded demurely down the road towards his field, I could have sworn there was now a gleam on his eye and a lightness in his step that hadn't been there before. It was as if he'd been rejuvenated.

"Ah!" said Mr Gray when I returned the head collar and told him about it "It would have been the sound of the lawn mower that did it. You think about it; to him it could have sounded like people clapping. A lot of people and just what he would have been used to when he'd finished his act in the ring. And he'd have been trained to rear up on to his back legs and to acknowledge it." After that, I never again tried to kick him into action. Why should he, after all? He deserved his retirement.

My only other experience with horses that winter was when I followed the hunt — on my bicycle. The meet was at Brill, and I decided to take a day's leave and follow it to the best of my ability. I knew one of the local farmers, John Rose, quite well and was pleased to see him there, mounted on a very large horse — he was a very large man. As the hunt moved off, he turned in his saddle and said, "You follow me, my duck!" I was surprised — did he know something I didn't? Did he, with his knowledge of the countryside know exactly where hounds would find? It seemed unlikely, but I decided to give him the benefit of the doubt. Keeping a respectful distance behind, I followed the enormous rump of his horse and those of two of his farmer friends, down a lane and away from the rest of the field. I soon found out where we were going — to the nearest pub! Once there, they all dismounted, and I did the same. Seconds later, I was being presented with the bridles of their mounts and assured that "they'll be no trouble, my duck! And we won't forget you!" And then they disappeared into the pub, and I was left staring up the nostrils of three of the most enormous horses I had ever seen who, to give them their due, did nothing more frightening than an occasional shake of their heads. And, to give John and his friends their due also, they didn't forget me. Every time they had a gin, they sent one out to me. When they eventually rejoined me, the number of horses I was holding had doubled!

And that, as far as I was concerned, ended my day's "hunting". I did try to catch them up as they trotted away down the lane, and I did, indeed, manage to mount my bike. But ride it? Not a chance! After I'd fallen into the ditch for the third time, I gave up and pushed it home. And that was the ignominious end of my day of "riding to hounds"! Not quite what I'd expected, but it did make a good story!

218

I remember that there were several heavy falls of snow that winter. It sat on top of the windmill for days, looking rather like a rakish beret as it slowly disintegrated, and lingered on the field that sloped away from the cottage, inspiring my landlord to dig out his skis and traverse it in long, ever increasing swoops that made me green with envy. The village children shot down the hillocks on the Common on tin trays or homemade toboggans, screaming at the tops of their voices. Sydney and Betty made a huge punch bowl of mulled wine and invited me round to taste it. And my mother came to stay.

She was still searching for her country cottage and had already made several abortive and expensive dashes up from Swansea to view properties that I had thought might be suitable. In the end, I suggested that she put her furniture into store, came to stay with me and looked around at her leisure.

My landlord was quite agreeable to the idea and so, in mid-November, my mother moved in — plus the piano that had cost £41 way back in the nineteen twenties and which she had cherished ever since. Apparently, it would require specialist attention if it went into storage which my mother feared it wouldn't receive, unless she paid out vast sums of money. It would be much more sensible if it came to stay with us. Once more, my landlord voiced no objection, and it arrived, so to speak, by "special delivery" with the deliverymen playing a tune on it when it reached the garden gate, just to prove it was still in working order. For the next few months, it occupied a large part of the living room but proved useful, once my mother had covered its top with a cloth, as a sort of halfway house for dirty dishes en route for the kitchen.

Naturally, my life changed considerably after my mother arrived. Admittedly, with two small bedrooms, it was difficult for me to have friends to stay, but I was now coming home most evenings to a hot meal in a warm cottage. As well as having lifts with him, I was now seeing Tony in the evenings and at the weekends, and he was always willing to take my mother and me to view any prospective cottages we heard of. But my mother seemed in no hurry to go, and we settled into a routine that suited us both. In spite of the cramped living conditions, my father would occasionally come down from London for the weekend but was quite happy to leave cottage-hunting to my mother.

When summer came again, Tony and I would often go off to Abbotsbury, in Dorset, for the weekend to a guesthouse on the Chesil Beach, run by Hilda and Harry, cousins of his. It was made up of a row of five old coastguard cottages, separated from the beach by only a grassy bank. A rowing boat was kept permanently pulled up on the shingle, and taking this out gave us hours of enjoyment. It was magic to lie in bed at night and be lulled to sleep by the rhythmic crunch of the waves on the shingle.

If Hilda was busy "doing teas" — as she did at weekends — we would help out, waiting at table. I greatly enjoyed standing there, taking orders and trying to look and sound professional, while Tony carried out the trays. Occasionally, we would even be left a tip which we would spend in the evenings when we all drove out to a pub somewhere in the hinterland where we drank very rough, very cheap cider. I could only manage half a pint, but Tony, most unwisely, couldn't resist having more and, on more than one occasion, had to be escorted into the back garden by the landlord where he was violently sick behind a hedge. For this service, Tony felt obliged to tip him half a crown — roughly equivalent to 25p. Meanly, I wondered if the landlord ran a profitable sideline providing the same service to other visitors. I noticed several knowing nods and winks among the regulars when Tony, somewhat pale of cheek, came back.

That summer of 1951, I decided I would use my summer holiday to visit Bill's grave in Tunisia. I managed it through the good offices of the Ramblers' Society, a travel company that specialized in walking holidays but, on this occasion, was organizing one mostly by coach, although some walking would be involved. With an extraordinary piece of luck, I discovered that the route would actually pass by the gates of the war cemetery at Enfidaville where Bill had eventually been buried. I wrote to the Ramblers and asked if it would be possible for the coach to stop there for a few minutes while I found the grave and took photographs for my parents.

In reply, they sent me the names and addresses of the two leaders on the holiday — Ron Swell and Richard Carstairs — and suggested I write to them direct. This, I did and received back the excellent news that not only would they make sure the coach stopped at the cemetery, they would also arrange for me to meet the head of the Imperial War Graves Commission in Tunisia, an RAF Wing Commander, based in Tunis who would be able to give me the exact location of the grave in the cemetery so that I would be able to go straight to it.

We weren't scheduled to pick up our coach until we reached Tunis, where we would also acquire our French guide and a party of French tourists. The British contingent was due to assemble at 8.30a.m. at Victoria Station, London on Friday, July 25th. Having spent the previous night with Heather and Dennis at Harrow, I turned up at Victoria bright and early and wearing a summer dress, a large, straw sunhat and sandals. To my astonishment, the other members of the party already assembled looked as if they were going on an immediate safari. They wore shorts or long trousers in varying shades of khaki, topped either by khaki shirts or camouflage jackets. Long socks and desert boots were *de rigeur*. All that was missing were the pith helmets. Growing more and more worried, I lingered on the outskirts of the group; clearly, my attire was completely out of place.

And then, to my great relief, a girl of about my age suddenly appeared at my side, looking even more summery than me. Her straw hat actually sported an artificial poppy or two on its brim and was tied under her chin — her dress was even longer and fuller-skirted than mine. On her feet were sandals practically identical to mine. We took one look at each other and then at the assembled throng, raised our eyebrows and said as one, "Coffee?"

And this, we did, leaving our rucksacks — we did, at least, have these in common with everyone else — on top of the ever-growing pile. There was still ten minutes to go before the actual rendezvous time — just enough for a quick dash to the nearest coffee bar.

Her name was Sheila; a couple of years younger than me, she'd recently graduated from St. Andrew's University and was now working in the library of some esoteric literary foundation of which I'd never heard. She lived in a London suburb with her invalid mother.

It didn't take us long to exchange biographical details and to agree that the rest of the party seemed to be a right collection of goons. We drank our coffee in a few scalding gulps, and I swear we were no more than one minute late getting back to the rendezvous point to find everyone gone and our rucksacks left in the middle of the concourse for anyone to pinch. Righteous indignation! Couldn't they have waited just one more minute? In hindsight — why on earth should they? However — "Goons!" we muttered to each other and found our own way to the boat train departure platform and the compartments that had been reserved for us and where we met up with our leaders who — rather disturbingly! — were wearing khaki shorts but with the saving grace of checked shirts.

Of course, once we got to know them, the "goons" turned out to be really nice people and with a sprinkling of "characters". The one I remember particularly was a woman — slightly older than me —

called Liz who had been an officer in the ATS but still managed not to be bossy and had the saving grace, as far as Sheila and I were concerned, of appearing at bedtime in a flame-coloured chiffon nightie that was definitely "one-up" on the service issue pyjamas that I was still wearing. Most of our accommodation was in Youth Hostel dormitories, so we knew all about each other's nightwear. As befitted Liz's worldly status, she knew of a Parisian night club to which she took us all that night. It was, of course, situated on the Left Bank and in a cellar reached by a flight of poorly-lit stone steps.

After she'd greeted "monsieur le Patron" with the customary embrace of old friends and effusive kisses on both cheeks, we were seated in a very dark corner and entertained by a Jean Sablon look-alike. The drinks, needless to say, were rather expensive, but we all relaxed and got to know each other better.

Next day, we caught a train down to Marseilles where we were to stay overnight at a hotel in the dock area before embarking for Tunis. After supper, Ron told us that if we wanted to "go out on the town", he didn't advise us to do it on our own and certainly not to leave the Canabiere, the main road through the harbour. Nobody was tempted to do that, certainly not among the women, and Ron was able to count us all back in long before midnight.

The crossing to Tunis was a mixed blessing; certainly it was a lovely day, and before long we were all stretched out on deck and soaking up the sunshine. Besides passengers, we had a cargo of oranges on board, and one of the boxes just happened to have broken open so that its contents were now spilling over the deck — but not for long. Everyone's Vitamin C intake rose dramatically!

The crossing lasted overnight and, in our case, this meant sleeping on deck. Not that anyone minded; the air was balmy, there was a plentiful supply of blankets and there was a nearly full moon. The only downside was that the toilet was rapidly becoming unusable. Sheila and I must have been well on the way to becoming dehydrated because we resolutely refused to drink any more liquid although the oranges must have helped. Even so, it was a great relief, in more ways than one, to arrive in Tunis and have the benefit of a spanking new Youth Hostel where the toilets doubled as showers.

Tunis was sweltering and after a visit to the Roman remains at Carthage, further down the coast, we bathed at La Marsa. For the duration of our holiday, we seemed to spend more time in the Mediterranean than out of it, especially in the late evening.

We had now joined up with our French contingent of holiday makers with their guide, a vivacious little French girl called Yvonne. We didn't fraternize to any great extent, but we did have extremely noisy sing-songs on the coach when each nationality would vie with the other for the highest level of decibels . . . Our speciality was "Old MacDonald had a farm . . ."

On our second day in Tunis, I went to see Wing Commander Humphries; a charming man who told me exactly where to find Bill's grave. We were scheduled to reach Enfidaville early on the fourth day of our tour; when the coach drew up outside the cemetery gates at about 7.30a.m., I was the only one to get off — no-one else had much stomach for visiting graves so early in the morning. I was glad of this for, apart from a couple of Arab gardeners quietly going about their tasks, I was quite alone and able to stand for as long as I wanted beside Bill's grave before I took my box Brownie out of its case and took a couple of photographs. It was very peaceful with hardly a sound except for the rustle of a gentle breeze among the leaves of the eucalyptus trees that grew at the edges of the cemetery. Every grave was immaculately cared for and every evening, Wing Commander Humphries had told me, the Last Post would be sounded and every morning, the Reveille. Much comforted by the visit, for I had always tried to follow Bill wherever he went, I went back to the coach where everyone gave me sympathetic smiles but didn't try to talk to me, for which I was most grateful. Later that day, we passed a signpost to Mareth, and I swear that I felt Bill's presence.

It was a good holiday in spite of it being so hot that our driver did, one midday, actually fry an egg on the bonnet of the coach! We rested up at midday, swam whenever possible but still managed to visit catacombs, caves where troglodytes lived very happily, wonderfully preserved Roman amphitheatres far out in the desert and oases where camels drank their fill from deep, silent pools. Even the French Foreign Legion popped up, on manoeuvres in the desert but having a break in a bar that we had gone into. On one occasion, we shared an enormous platter of couscous with a Bedouin tribe; we all sat round in a circle and dug in with our bare hands. At Hammamet, I remember, we slept on the beach, within sound of the sea. And there wasn't a vestige of a towering hotel block in sight. Amazingly, we did sometimes walk, and I have recorded climbing a mountain behind a Berber village with wonderful views from the summit.

The highlight of our holiday, we had been promised, would be a couple of days on the Island of Djerba; golden sands, blue sea, shady palms — the perfect place in which to relax before the journey home. But there was one thing the blurb forgot to mention — scorpions, whose sting could be deadly. They had the habit of lurking in the most unlikely places, like inside your shoes or between the creases of the clothes you took off before bed. I don't know about the rest of the party, but for Sheila and me, they were a nightmare . . . even though we never actually saw one. Also, there seemed to be a lot of construction work going on, as the island prepared to turn itself into one of the major tourist attractions of the Mediterranean; no doubt, by now, they've persuaded the scorpions to go elsewhere!

However, we certainly made the most of our last day in Tunis; shopping in the souks occupied most of our time. I bought some very pretty pottery, but my pride and joy was a big pitcher — the sort that Rebecca, in the Bible story, balanced on her shoulder on her way to the well. It would, I thought, look perfect on the sill of the living-room window in the cottage. The fact that it had cost only the equivalent of one shilling in English money seemed to make it doubly precious. From then on, I cherished it as if it were the Crown Jewels; all the way across the Mediterranean to Marseilles and then on the train back to Paris, I sat with it either on my lap or, if I was lying down, immediately beside me. Soon, I was being referred to as Pat the Pot! Even when we all hung over the rails of the ship to watch a shoal of flying fish, I made sure it was safely anchored inside a lifebelt. As I did when we eventually crossed the Channel and had to endure a very rough crossing. At Waterloo, I bade Sheila a fond farewell but arranged to meet her in London in a fortnight's time. In spite of my initial impressions, everyone in the party had turned out to be very good company, and I was sorry to leave them. I had already arranged to stay overnight with Barbara when I got back to Oxford but would be going back to the cottage in the evening, so I took my pot into the office with me. And it was then that ruin loomed. Walking into the office, I caught my foot on the doorsill and fell forward. You can guess the rest! I was almost in tears by the time I reached my desk, still clutching the pieces.

However, it had broken into four large pieces and these a kind colleague was able to glue back together. So, after all, it did end up on my window sill where its history made a very good story for many months to come. Sadly, it met its demise early one morning when I'd carelessly left the window open all night and an inquisitive horse, put out to graze in the field, put its head through at first light and nudged it on to the floor

228

where it shattered into so many pieces it was quite impossible to mend.

Soon after that holiday, my mother found her cottage. It was in a village called Stewkley, a few miles outside Leighton Buzzard and was advertised in the paper for the princely sum of £325 — remember, this was 1950. We rang the contact number — it was that of a solicitor in Aylesbury who was acting for the vendor — and made an appointment to collect the key from him, and I took the day off.

It was an ancient, 17th century cottage with a thatched roof, a beamed ceiling, a vast inglenook and a small, but adequate, front garden. Although it would need quite a bit of refurbishment — it hadn't, for instance, a bathroom and the doorless opening between the two bedrooms was so small, we had to bend double to get through it — it more than satisfied my mother's requirements, particularly the price. Later, we discovered that a member of the Pankhurst family, who had played such an important role in the suffragette movement, had once occupied it.

Cock-a-hoop, we returned to Aylesbury, and my mother, who always had an eye for a bargain, made an offer of £320. I held my breath. It seemed to be tempting Providence to offer less than the asking price when it was already so low. The solicitor thought so, too, and with a charming smile — he obviously liked the look of my mother — he assured her that his client would only accept the full asking price. So, she offered the full price and the deal was struck.

Even more cock-a-hoop, we left the office and went in search of food — we hadn't eaten since an early breakfast. We soon found it but lingered too long over the meal and discovered, to our horror, that we had missed the last bus that would give us a connection to Thame and a lift home from Tony.

There was only one thing for it — we would have to hitch! But doing it in uniform in wartime and doing it in peacetime with your mother were two very different things. However, in the event, it couldn't have been easier. The first lorry driver was so intrigued at the sight of us — my mother was brandishing her handbag instead of her thumb! — he was laughing like a drain when he screeched to a halt. It took quite a lot of heaving on my part and pulling on his to get her up into his cab, and she got a fit of the giggles halfway up. But in the end, we made it. She then proceeded to tell the driver exactly what we'd been doing, and he was so tickled that when we finally reached Thame, he insisted upon getting out and helping her down. After that episode, she had to be actively discouraged from standing at the roadside rather than tamely waiting for a bus, even though one was due!

That night, Tony and I took her to the pub to celebrate her purchase and, to make it all perfect, Tony was able to recommend a couple of builders living in Brill who proved happy to take on the job of restoring the cottage and putting in a bathroom.

But it was not only my mother who was now hoping to begin a new life. For some time now, I had been interested in trying to transfer to what was loosely known as Welfare. The Ministry at Oxford had its own welfare officer and an assistant. They came under the auspices of a chief welfare officer, as did several other regional welfare officers and those who looked after various Ministry offices in London. The old Carlton Hotel at the bottom of Haymarket, being a relatively small office, was staffed by a Clerical Officer under the guidance of an executive officer who was housed in the building where the minister had his office. Because a female Clerical Officer had left to get married, a vacancy had come up in the Carlton. Due to the Oxford welfare officer, Eileen Quelch, kindly putting my name forward, I was asked to go up to London for an interview with the chief welfare officer.

Although I had made many visits to London since that first, precarious crossing of it during the war, I had only been to visit friends in the suburbs; I'd never been part of the work force. Although wearing my smartest dress, I arrived in the Metropolis, bare-legged, sandals on my feet and certainly not wearing gloves. Gloves? In mid-summer? Only a traffic policeman did that! But the London streets seemed to be teeming with women of all ages, and not only were they wearing stockings on their legs and little white gloves on their hands, they sported high-heeled sandals on their feet and still managed to move twice as fast as we did in Oxford. They were almost keeping up with the buses, of which there were thousands! But I had been well briefed and managed to catch the right one and arrived at my interview on time.

There seemed to be no other candidates and, after a few relevant questions and a general chat, I was offered the job. Of course, I took it and went back to Brill to tell my mother, feeling extremely pleased with myself. So elated was I that I committed the almost mortal sin, even then, of digging up a cowslip from the embankment at tiny Ludgershall station when no-one was looking, to take home to my mother. She was particularly fond of cowslips. And so, a few weeks later, my long association with Oxford, in one way or another, was over. Having this section on the end seems to negate the feeling of finality.

Now, I live near enough to visit sometimes and although the shopping malls become more and more extensive, parking more and more difficult and you have to pay to visit the Botanical Gardens, it still remains quintessentially the same. Three years in the Potato and Carrot Division of the Ministry of Agriculture, Fisheries and Food were, in my humble opinion, just as enjoyable as three at Christ Church or Balliol as a student!

Epilogue

I am writing this in Abergavenny in a charming apartment in a house called Tyn-y-Bryn that is halfway up the Deri. There is a magnificent view across the valley to the Skirrid, or Holy Mountain as it's sometimes called. The sun rises behind the mountain, and on a clear morning it is worth getting up early to see. I have stayed here many times with Chris and Sandra Belcham who own Tyn-y-Bryn and who offer as much hospitality to their canine visitors as they do to their owners.

Abergavenny has changed very little in the past sixty or so years; when a town is surrounded by steep hills, there is little that the developers can do. They have in-filled, of course, wherever possible, and there is now a bungalow in the garden where Bill and I used to climb our separate pear trees. But both the houses we lived in look exactly the same, although the monkey-puzzle tree has gone.

My old school is now a Youth Hostel, and the Grammar School and the Girls' Intermediate have been combined into one big Comprehensive. Mrs. Hibbert's, where we bought our sticks of liquorice and sherbert fountains, is now a pretty little private house. The saddest change for me is that Llwyni Lane is now part of a big housing estate, but I am not sad at all that there is now no bathing area on the banks of the Usk. In fact, it would be dangerous for anyone to bathe in it these days, the currents are so treacherous. But Castle Meadows, which border the river, is now a popular area for dog walkers. On a clear day, and preferably in spring, before the trees become too dense with foliage, the view from the river bank is superb; there is the square tower of the Castle keep, the copper spire of the Town Hall and beyond, the panorama of the mountains that, short of an earthquake, will never change. In summer, as it is now, the river banks are swathes of colour with the pink and mauve of balsam and thistle and the creamy panacles of hemlock and meadowsweet. My little dog, Milo, explores every inch of it.

There are many improvements in the town; the centre of it has either been turned into a traffic-free precinct or a one-way system leading into a bypass created from existing roads so that few buildings have had to be pulled down. St. Mary's church and its ancient Priory have had a miraculous face-lift, and inside the church, I was very proud to find Bill's name in the Book of Remembrance for those killed in the last war. Sadly, none of my old friends are still here, but Peg Powell — or "Peggy Knees-Up" as my father called her — is alive and well and living in Devon, where I visit her every year. This summer, I have visited Stella Powell, sister of Susie who was one of my class mates, and she has brought me up to date on what has happened to old friends.

Of my old WAAF friends, Margaret and William have died, but their children and grandchildren prosper, and I receive regular news. The last I heard of Heather, she had gone to live with her daughter in Cornwall.

But — a great bonus — I have made several good friends in the WAAF Association, a branch of which meets regularly in Milton Keynes. We meet every month for lunch and a chat and we have some hairy tales to tell. Several of them have given talks in schools about their experiences — much to the children's astonishment. Was that fragile old lady sitting with her stick in front of them really once in charge of a barrage balloon? Or took an aircraft engine apart and put it back together again? Of one thing we are all quite certain — we wouldn't have missed it for anything.

I recently revisited Benson; the airfield is still there and is still operational, although our married quarters have been replaced by newer models. The bare bones of the village are still the same, but houses have multiplied, and the canteen is long gone. There is a filling station where the Riverside café used to be, but Cherry Trees is still there and so is the pub next door, the "Home Sweet Home", now a much smarter establishment than the little country pub where we would sometimes quaff our half pints of cider on a summer evening. Nowadays, you can get a very good meal there.

Dorchester-upon-Thames, with its ancient Abbey and mediaeval houses is now, fortunately, by-passed and has lost none of its charm. And Wittenham Clumps can still be climbed, although, inevitably, at a much slower pace than before, and there is now a car waiting for me at the bottom to get me home and not a bicycle called George!

Of the friends I made in Oxford immediately after the war, Margaret, with whom I had such a wonderful holiday in Italy, is now in a nursing home in Scotland but is still enjoying life and the exploits of her children and grandchildren. We speak on the telephone regularly. Barbara now lives in Gloucestershire, and I see her every few months. I lost touch with Andy but know that he and Ian and Eric all made successful careers in medicine.

Brill isn't far away from where I live now, and I often meet up with Mary, the sister of a nice man who would sometimes give us a lift into Oxford in the back of his sports car. Because no building is allowed on the Common, there has been no massive development. The windmill is still there and now cared for by a group of enthusiasts. You could also say that my cottage is still there but it has now been incorporated into the main cottage and been thoroughly refurbished. The coal shed has gone along with Ellie's shed. However, it is still the end bump of a very wavy roof-line. I'm very glad that it's now part of the whole because otherwise I would probably want to live there again and it wouldn't be the same without Sydney and Betty in the village. Sadly, Betty died when she was still quite young, but Sydney made a very happy second marriage to Monica and lived in a large house on the Common until he died.

236

And me? I now live very happily in sheltered accommodation in Buckinghamshire with my little dog and not far from a caring stepson and his wife and three delightful grandchildren. Milo and I enjoy excellent country walks most days and while my marching days are most definitely over, I now have the perfect excuse for leaning on my stick and enjoying the view. It's very relaxing being of a certain age, and I can thoroughly recommend it.

Also available in ISIS Large Print:

A Bethnal Green Memoir

Derek Houghton

"There was once a street in Bethnal Green. How I wish that street were still there . . . to be able to return once in a while, to stand in the street where I grew up. To look at the houses and the people who lived in them, and to bring back the memories of my boyhood."

Derek Houghton gives a colourful insight into life as a real "East Ender". The memories recalled openly by the author give a snapshot of community characterised by contrasts. Neighbourliness and community spirit were highly valued, yet whole families often found themselves turned out onto the streets by ruthless landlords.

The war provided a sudden rupture, for both the author and his neighbourhood. The relative peace of his time as an evacuee in Oxfordshire contrasts strongly with the destruction of Bethnal Green when the bombs rained down.

ISBN 978-0-7531-9552-9 (hb)
ISBN 978-0-7531-9553-6 (pb)

Hops, Doodlebugs and Floods

Dr Alan Whitcomb

"You always wore old clothes while hop picking as they got stained and smelly from the hops. My pride of attire from the hopping box during my early teens was a pair of horse riding jodhpurs."

This is the tale of a boy born into a typical East End of London family during the Blitz. The author narrates his story with nostalgia and humour, beginning with his early memories of living in Essex and hop picking in Kent, before moving on to life in the 1950s and the devastating east coast floods of 1953.

After leaving school at 15 Alan joined the Merchant Navy illegally. He grew up quickly as he sailed the world, had a brush with danger during the Suez Crisis, suffered appendicitis while sailing down the coast of Africa, and spent a spell in an Australian prison!

ISBN 978-0-7531-9554-3 (hb)
ISBN 978-0-7531-9555-0 (pb)

Growing up in Sussex

Gerry Wells

"Rescued by Father, probably startled from his newspaper, I was handed dripping and yelling over the fence to be sorted out by Mother who wouldn't have been amused. A second baptism perhaps, just to make sure."

This compelling memoir starts with a boy's journey through the early years of the 1930s — days of the rag and bone man, street lamplighters and in the background, Hitler. Then life gets real, at school where cane and cricket bat rule and even more real with army call-up and training.

In 1944/45 comes the crunch of combat in Operation Overlord. And after all that, with his ears still ringing a bit, comes the blessed call of demob and a taste of new delights, finding a woman daft enough to marry him before settling near his work on a farm to start his life as a man.

ISBN 978-0-7531-9540-6 (hb)
ISBN 978-0-7531-9541-3 (pb)

Suburban Boy

Adrian Bristow

"It was while we lived in Herbert Road that I acquired my toy box . . . It was quite large enough for me to climb into and it became by turns a boat, a cave or a house, according to which story or character was exercising my imagination at the time."

Suburban Boy is the charming story of a bygone era, of a boy who grew up in south-east London in the 1930s. Adrian Bristow came from that great unsung mass — the lower middle-class. He grew up in the years before the war, which saw the Depression, the Abdication, the rise of Hitler and the coming of war. It was also a time of rising standards of living, burgeoning home ownership, social mobility and the emergence of first-generation graduates. It was a time when there was respect for authority and a strong consciousness of nation and empire.

ISBN 978-0-7531-9538-3 (hb)
ISBN 978-0-7531-9539-0 (pb)